*For sons Steve Weber and Scott Weber, who grew up
to be amiable companions as well as excellent canoeists,
and who are now passing along the family passion
for riding rivers to their own children.*

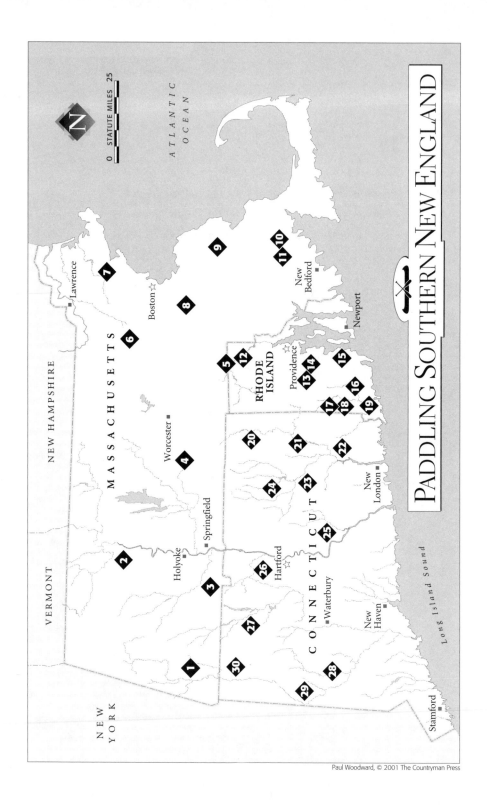

PADDLING SOUTHERN NEW ENGLAND

Paddling Southern New England

Paddling Southern New England

30 Canoe Trips in Massachusetts, Rhode Island, and Connecticut

Second Edition

Ken Weber

BACKCOUNTRY GUIDES
WOODSTOCK, VERMONT

An Invitation to the Reader

Rivers are notorious rearrangers of themselves and the objects they touch. Remember as you use this guide that water depths can vary considerably even from week to week, and that with time dams wash out, storms and floods rearrange rocks and channels, and new bridges and roads alter access points.

If you run these rivers and find them changed from their descriptions here, please let the author and publisher know so that corrections can be made in future editions. Other comments and suggestions for additional river trips are also welcome. Address all correspondence to:

Editor
Backcountry Guides
P.O. Box 748
Woodstock, VT 05091

Library of Congress Cataloging-in-Publication Data

Weber, Ken.
Paddling southern New England : 30 canoe trips in Massachusetts, Rhode Island, and Connecticut / Ken Weber. —2nd ed.
p. cm.
Rev. ed. of: Canoeing Massachusetts, Rhode Island, and Connecticut. c1980.
ISBN 0-88150-471-8 (alk. paper)
1. Canoes and canoeing—New England—Guidebooks. 2. Rivers—New England—Guidebooks. 3. New England—Guidebooks. I. Weber, Ken. Canoeing Massachusetts, Rhode Island, and Connecticut. II. Title.
GV776.N35 W42 2001
917.4—dc21   00-069122

Published by Backcountry Guides
A division of The Countryman Press
P.O. Box 748, Woodstock, Vermont 05091

Distributed by W.W. Norton & Company, Inc.
500 Fifth Avenue, New York, NY 10110

Interior design by Faith Hague
Cover design by Faith Hague
Cover photograph © David Brownell
Interior photographs by Kenneth J. Weber
Maps by Paul Woodward, © The Countryman Press

Excerpt on page 11 reprinted with permission from *Beyond Your Doorstep: A Handbook to the Country,* by Hal Borland, © 1962, Alfred A. Knopf, Inc.

Printed in the United States of America
10 9 8 7 6 5 4 3

Contents

Connecticut   121

Acknowledgments

CANOEING REQUIRES congenial partners, and writing a regional canoeing book requires many cooperative contacts. Fortunately, in this project, I found many people both willing and able to help. Most thanks go to my own family, my wife, Bettie, who paddled more of these rivers with me than anybody else, and our sons, Scott Weber and Steve Weber, who joined me when they could. Also of great help and appreciated companionship were good friends Ginny Leslie and the Points, Gary and Judianne, and their son, Bryant.

Providing valuable assistance, either by letting me join their group trips or in supplying information, were Bill Rush, Linda Pease, and Bev Thomas of the Narragansett Chapter of the Appalachian Mountain Club (AMC); Eric Stones, Kent Stivers, Polly Roberts, and Paul Sapia of the Connecticut AMC; David Miller of the Worcester Chapter of AMC; Steve Harrington of the Rhode Island Canoe and Kayak Association; and such organizations as the Farmington River Watershed Association, the Blackstone Valley National Heritage Corridor Commission, and others, some of whom helped merely by creating Internet web sites filled with information. To everybody involved, thank you.

Introduction

Any river is really the summation of a whole valley.
It shapes not only the land but the life and even the
culture of that valley. The trees that grow on its banks and
all the greenness there may be common elsewhere but they
still are special to that river. So are the birds, the insects,
the animals that live along that river's banks. And the
river has its own swarming life, its fish, its
amphibians, its reptiles. To think of any river as nothing
but water is to ignore the greater part of it.

—Hal Borland, Beyond Your Doorstep

THE FIRST EDITION OF THIS BOOK was published 20 years ago. It was meant for those who share a fascination for moving waters, and the same holds true for this second edition. Whether you prefer tranquil streams or roaring whitewater rivers, you are kindred souls. The lure to follow that water, to float with it around the next bend, is irresistible.

Canoes provide that opportunity. However, the same problems seem to plague every canoeist—where to go and what to expect? You may be looking for a soothing day watching the birds along some quiet river, or you may want an exhilarating couple of hours shooting rapids. But most of all, you want to know what lies ahead. Having to carry around dams you didn't know existed can rob a trip of much of its enjoyment, and running into unexpected rapids can be very dangerous, especially for family groups or inexperienced canoeists. In addition, there is the headache of having to search for the best places to launch and take out your canoe. Many canoeists have wasted half their trip day on such details.

This book's purpose is the same as the original edition's: to answer those questions. In updating this book, my companions and I returned to all the rivers in the original *Canoeing Massachusetts, Rhode Island, and Connecticut* and ended up substituting new trips for several of those runs and adding some others, making a total of 30 trips in this edition instead of the 25 in the first book. Some changes in trip descriptions were necessary because put-ins or take-outs have changed, different landmarks are now prominent, or other pertinent information was required. Occasionally, we changed the length of trips to make them more accommodating for family groups or beginning paddlers. In still other cases, we simply found new trips that we liked more than some of the originals. We tried even harder this time to choose trips without difficult obstacles, keeping portages to a minimum and selecting the most convenient access points, while including the most interesting and appealing segments of the rivers. We also added a few up-and-back trips this time for solo paddlers or those who prefer not to take two vehicles on their canoe trips.

As before, details are provided not only for put-ins, take-outs, and the type of canoeing to expect, but also on the distance you'll be traveling, how long the trip should take you, the best time of year to make the trip, and what you are likely to see along the way. Sketch maps and photographs also accompany the trip descriptions to help you in your planning.

The charts that precede each trip show you at a glance what you generally can expect on that trip. In addition to the recommended put-ins and take-outs I have listed some alternate access points so that you can plan shorter trips if necessary. Read the charts horizontally, following each line from the recommended put-in through the take-out point to the mileage and approximate paddling time. The last two categories at the far right show what kind of water conditions you can expect and the number of portages, if any, that you will encounter. The second line, then, shows similar information for what is usually a longer trip, most often starting from the same put-in but extending to a more distant take-out.

An example:

Put-in Point	Take-out Points	Approximate Distance	Approximate Trip Time	Condition of Water	Portages
Riverton picnic area	CT 318	4½ miles	2 hours	Minor rapids, smooth stretches	None
Riverton picnic area	Just above US 44 bridge	9½ miles	4–4½ hours	Minor rapids, smooth stretches, then mostly riffles	None

This chart, for the upper Farmington River in Connecticut, shows that a trip from the picnic area in Riverton to the CT 318 bridge covers 4½ miles and should take you about 2 hours. The water features both minor rapids and smooth stretches. There are no portages. If a longer trip appeals to you, look at the second line. It shows that a journey from the same spot in Riverton to a take-out just above the US 44 bridge covers 9½ miles and should take about 4 to 4½ hours. The additional miles of water are mostly riffles. Again, there are no portages.

Which Rivers?

All parts of southern New England are represented. There are 11 trips in Massachusetts, 11 in Connecticut, and 8 in Rhode Island. On these trips you can travel on the cold, clean streams descending from the Berkshires or float on sea-scented tidal rivers; you can follow the routes of Thoreau in northeastern Massachusetts or enjoy the wild water in western Connecticut; and you can paddle beside sleek powerboats in eastern Rhode Island or move a few miles west and glide through a junglelike swamp.

How Far? How Long Will It Take?

The rivers were chosen for the variety they offer in geography, types of canoeing, and shoreline attractions. These are trips designed for fun; they are not endurance tests. Each trip can be completed in a few hours.

The estimates of the time each trip should take are based on my own experiences on these rivers. Your time could be much faster or slower, depending on your interests, water conditions at the time you go, and what lures you to stop along the way. Generally, group trips take longer than trips involving just one or two canoes because of pauses to watch or assist newcomers and because groups usually take longer lunch breaks. Nearly all of the time estimates I have noted allow for lunch stops, which are integral parts of my own trips. In addition to trip time, be sure to allow time for car shuttling on one-way journeys. (Only two trips in this book, the upper Pawtuxet in Rhode Island and Hopeville Pond–Pachaug River in Connecticut, end where they begin, although several trips can be paddled both ways.) Leaving a car at the take-out, driving to the put-in, and later picking up both cars takes more time than most canoeists realize.

Safety Comes First: A Few Tips

Remember that this is a "where-to" guide, not a "how-to" book. It isn't necessary to be an expert canoeist to enjoy most of the trips recommended, but you should be familiar with basic canoeing skills and have a knowledge of safety rules. Canoeing courses are available in most communities, often through the American Red Cross, which also publishes canoeing booklets that emphasize safety. Common sense is as important as skill; don't attempt a whitewater river if you are a beginner in the sport.

If you are taking children along, it is wise to restrict your traveling to the calmer rivers. Insist that children remain seated at all times, limit your passengers (you should carry no more than two children or one adult in addition to you and your paddling partner), and be sure you know the swimming abilities of everyone in your canoe. Life preservers should be worn on all trips. Wetsuits—thick rubber suits worn next to the skin—should also be worn on whitewater trips because such trips of necessity must be made in early spring when the water is extremely cold. Wetsuits will help fend off the cold and reduce the threat of hypothermia—probably the greatest danger of early-spring canoeing

Life preservers should be worn on all trips.

in southern New England. In addition, keep extra paddles and a first-aid kit secured inside your canoe. Another tip I've found useful, particularly if the take-out point is not obvious, is to tie a flag or ribbon or some other indicator visible from the water at the landing when you leave your car. Most take-out points are apparent, but others are narrow paths not readily recognizable from the water. Always look over the take-out carefully before heading to your launch spot so that you'll know what to look for as you come downriver.

Reading and Rating the River

Most of the rivers included in this book are usually smooth, but water conditions change dramatically with sudden spring thaws and heavy rains. Rivers run higher and faster at these times, and they can be dangerous. Keep this in mind when planning a trip, and look over the water carefully at your put-in, at your take-out, and at as many points in between as possible before launching. Probably the best way to tell when a river is running at high-water stage is by checking the shoreline. If trees and bushes are standing in water, the water level is above normal. Consequently, a trip on it may vary considerably from my description. Conversely, when the shoreline vegetation is some distance from the water, the river is abnormally low. This situation can cause another set of problems. You may run aground or get hung up on rocks, and spend as much time walking your canoe as paddling. You can check the Internet—an invaluable service not available when the first edition of this book was published—to find water conditions on most rivers by using the United States Geological Survey water-flow site (http://water.usgs.gov), which is updated daily. Many local watershed associations and canoe clubs also have their own web sites and can provide useful information. A little research can save you both time and headaches.

Dams and water releases also play a major role in fluctuating water levels on the rivers. The fastest-moving rivers in particular are subject to great variations in the amount of water being released, which in turn depends upon power requirements. As a general rule, more water is released on weekdays than on weekends, with the smallest flowage usually on Sundays, when power requirements are smallest. Major power companies will often supply a schedule of water releases on the larger rivers.

I have tried to indicate which rivers can be run through the drier summer months and which are strictly spring rivers. All the whitewater trips are best made long before summer arrives because the rivers become extremely shallow later in the season. On the whitewater runs, I have chosen sections that are exciting and scenic but have omitted the more dangerous stretches. I have used the same ratings for the rapids on these runs as those used by the American Canoe Association, the Appalachian Mountain Club, and most other prominent canoeing organizations.

In these ratings, Class I is moving water with some riffles, small waves, and few or no obstacles. Class II indicates small-scale rapids where there are wide channels that are obvious without scouting from shore. Class III rapids should be scouted—they are capable of swamping canoes. They have high, irregular waves that arise from water running through narrow, twisting passages. Only a few of the rivers in this book—the upper Farmington, the Shepaug, the Salmon, and possibly the faster stretch of the Housatonic or part of the Deerfield—generate Class III rapids, and then only under abnormal conditions. Class IV and Class V rapids are for expert canoeists only; therefore, no river trips that would involve such sections have been included here.

My wife, sons, assorted friends, and I have spent the last two years canoeing the rivers of southern New England to make these 30 selections. In general, we found them better than when photographer Larry Millard and I did the original book. Many of the access points have been improved, several of the rivers are considerably cleaner, there appears to be more wildlife—beavers in particular are a big part of the scene now—and there is more protection for these waterways, more pride taken by local communities in their appearance. In the first edition, I stated that in writing that book we discovered a fortune in canoeing enjoyment. These rivers are beautiful; they deserve to be recognized as such. I've paddled some of them often over the years, but others I've been on only a few times. Having revisited them, I now wonder why I didn't go back sooner. These rivers are still a treasure.

Summary of Canoeing Terms

Most technical canoeing terms were omitted from this book so beginning canoeists would find the descriptions relatively easy to understand. The following terms, however, are used. Knowing their meanings will make your reading more enjoyable and your canoeing safer.

Back eddy: The water immediately downstream from a boulder or other obstruction. The water is forced to swirl around the obstruction and flow momentarily upstream. These eddies are valuable on fast-moving rivers because you can use them for rest breaks or to check on following canoes.

Back-watering: The process of paddling backward, that is, against the current; a technique often used in fast water and rapids to slow down, turn, or stop.

Blowdown: A fallen tree in the river, usually at least partially blocking the canoe's path.

Bottom-scrapers: The term commonly used to describe rocks just below the water's surface.

Bow: The front end of a canoe.

Carry: Another word for portage; an obstacle (usually a dam) that cannot be canoed over or around. The canoe must be taken out of the water, carried around the obstacle, and launched again.

Channel: The route through the riverbed that carries the deepest water and the strongest currents.

Chute: A break in a ledge or dam that acts as a funnel for the water. Chutes are often, but not always, canoeable.

Current: The rate of flow in a river. Strong current means the water is moving very fast.

Deadwater: Refers to water that is not moving; usually associated with water just above a dam.

Downstream: The direction in which the water is flowing.

Draw stroke: A valuable technique in whitewater canoeing; refers to reaching out to the side of the canoe, plunging the paddle into the water, and pulling or drawing the paddle toward you. This, in effect, moves the canoe in the direction of your paddle. It is used to make quick, sharp maneuvers.

Eddy: The quiet water behind obstacles. Eddies are often used for taking rest breaks.

Flatwater: Refers to water, whether moving or still, that shows no signs of turbulence.

Headwind: Any wind blowing in the faces of the canoeists; a major problem when canoeing large ponds or very wide rivers.

Hung up: A term canoeists use for running aground on a sandbar or, more often, for being immobilized atop a rock in shallow water.

Landing: A spot on the shore from which canoes can easily be put in or taken out of the water.

Launching: The act of putting a canoe in the water.

Liftover: An obstacle, usually a fallen tree or log. It is passed by floating up to it, stepping out, and lifting the canoe over it.

Lining: A method of taking the canoe through extremely shallow water. Canoeists walk in the water or along the shore while allowing the empty canoe to float and keep control of the canoe by means of an attached rope or line.

Low water: Refers to a river's condition when the water level is unusually low; a situation common in summer and autumn.

Meander: A winding path; refers to rivers that curl back and forth in a wandering pattern.

Passage: A route or path; used in canoeing to refer to the way around an obstacle, such as the right or left passage around an island.

Portage: As a noun, refers to an impassable obstacle in the river; as a verb, refers to the act of taking the canoe out of the water, carrying it around the obstacle, and putting it back in the water.

Put-in: The spot from which you launch your canoe and begin a trip.

Quickwater: Refers to fast-moving water with some turbulence; not as severe as rapids or whitewater.

Rapids: Water cascading over rocks with the water flowing very fast and the rocks large enough and close enough together to create a roaring, sometimes dangerous turbulence.

Riffles: Water flowing over small rocks causing only minor turbulence or a "bumpy" surface.

Rock-dodging: Refers to maneuvering a canoe between rocks or boulders in the riverbed.

Scouting: Checking the water ahead, usually from shore; a prudent practice prior to canoeing rapids to decide which route to take.

Scratchy: Refers to rivers so shallow the canoe is likely to scrape rocks on the bottom, or be scratched, in passing.

Standing waves: Whitecapped waves of turbulent water caused by water pouring over a dam, boulder, or some other obstacle.

Stern: The back end of the canoe.

Swamping: Also sometimes called dumping; refers to the canoe being filled with water.

Take-out: The end of your trip; where you take the canoe out of the water.

Tides: The movement of ocean waters to land, or up rivers, and out again; in this book applicable only on the saltwater trips: the North River and the Pettaquamscutt (Narrow) River.

Upstream: The direction from which the water is flowing.

Wetsuit: A heavy rubber suit worn next to the skin for warmth when canoeing wild rivers in cold weather.

Whitewater: Refers to rivers on which the water flows over and around rocks with so much force that it creates a white foam.

PART I
Massachusetts

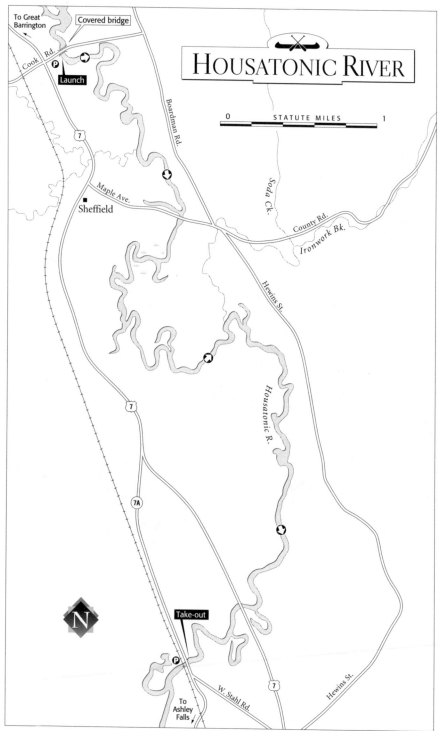

To Great
Barrington

Covered bridge

Cook Rd.

P
Launch

Boardman Rd.

HOUSATONIC RIVER

0   STATUTE MILES   1

Soda Ck.

County Rd.

Ironwork Bk.

Maple Ave.

■
Sheffield

7

Hewins St.

Housatonic R.

7

7A

N

Take-out

P

To
Ashley
Falls

W. Stahl Rd.

7

Hewins St.

1

Housatonic River

Sheffield to Ashley Falls

Put-in Point	Take-out Point	Approximate Distance	Approximate Trip Time	Condition of Water	Portages
Covered bridge, Sheffield	MA 7A	8 miles	3–4 hours	Smooth	None

This stretch of the Housatonic River in southwestern Massachusetts is great for a leisurely summertime paddle. Save it for June or July, when many other rivers are dwindling, and you may be in for a treat.

There are many segments of the long Housatonic that can be canoed, and two more are included in this book, a flatwater stretch that begins where this one ends and crosses into Connecticut, and a quick-water run entirely in Connecticut. This section includes some of the best features of the other two trips: a steady current to make paddling easy, plenty of open views of good scenery, and often a pleasing array of wildlife. As a bonus, there are no portages.

The trip begins at a covered bridge at the north end of the village of Sheffield and ends at the MA 7A bridge near Ashley Falls. By road, the distance is only 4 miles. By river, because of the numerous bends and turns, the distance is about 8 miles and can take between 3 and 4 hours, depending on current and your interest in exploring the backwaters and shorelines. The ambitious can easily extend the trip beyond MA 7A and do another segment of the Housatonic (see Trip 30) as well, but be aware that there are few good take-out points until reaching the dam at Falls Village, more than 10 miles from MA 7A. It may be better to paddle the two segments separately.

A rebuilt covered bridge is a great place to start a canoe trip.

The Housatonic can be done in almost any season, of course, but because it drains much of the Berkshire region, it tends to run high and fast in early spring. I recommend doing this segment in summer, so you can take your time and enjoy the float. There is often much to see. On a June trip here, my wife and I came upon a doe with a newborn fawn at the shore, discovered a large colony of bank swallows, saw numerous kingfishers, cormorants, and other birds, then finished beside a large farm where bobolinks were singing. We wouldn't have had such experiences on an April run.

Access

To leave a vehicle at the take-out, drive MA 7A to the bridge just north of Ashley Falls, a short distance above the Connecticut line. There is room to park at the north side of the bridge. The take-out is up a steep but short slope and over a guardrail. It is not a great take-out but better than those offered at other bridges in the area.

To drive to the put-in, follow MA 7A north until it merges with US 7, then follow US 7 into the village of Sheffield. Near the far end of the village, look for a sign for the Sheffield Covered Bridge, across from Cook Road. The covered bridge and the put-in are down a short lane to the right.

The River

Before launching, take some time to look over the covered bridge, a rebuilt version of one that had stood here from 1854 until burning in 1994. No cars can use the bridge, but visitors can walk onto it and get a feeling for what covered bridges were like.

The early segment is indicative of what most of the trip will feature: lots of curves and bends, many tall trees interspersed with open fields and meadows, and birds. In summer you'll see barn swallows, tree swallows, kingbirds, orioles, red-winged blackbirds, and probably several other species. There are likely to be blowdowns in the water, but throughout the trip the river is wide enough to make maneuvering past the logs and fallen trees an easy matter.

Keep an eye on the shoreline; you are likely to see many trails used by animals in visiting the river, and the many sandbars and muddy banks will show animal tracks ranging from wild turkeys and great blue herons to deer, raccoons, skunks, opossums, and muskrats. Some of the higher banks also have tunnels used as nesting places by kingfishers and bank swallows, although the best places for such nests are in the second half of this trip.

In 45 minutes or so you pass under your first bridge (poor access), then, for a brief time, the shores become more forested. Here, the trees are a featured attraction, many of them being huge oaks, maples, and sycamores that have seen the river flowing by for many, many decades. When the shorelines open again, you can see fields and some farm buildings in the distance, but almost none are close to the water. Beyond the farms the hills loom, adding to the bucolic setting. It was in this area where we nearly floated up to the deer with a speckled fawn that couldn't have been more than a few days old.

It is about 6 miles between bridges in this section, and most of it is very pretty, very curvy, and very easy. Most of the time, it's simply a matter of steering around bends. There are a couple of islands in the river, but in all but the lowest of water conditions there is plenty of room for passage.

Just as the next bridge comes into view (you may hear traffic before seeing the bridge), look on the left for a high bank with dozens of holes. On one trip here, we counted more than 50 nest tunnels made by bank swallows, cousins of the better-known tree and barn swallows. These brownish swallows filled the air as we passed; we could only imagine how many mosquitoes they gobble each summer.

It takes a while to reach the US 7 bridge after seeing it because the river makes another of its frequent oxbow loops. After floating under this bridge you are in the final leg of the trip. On the right is one of the better scenes of the day—long fields sloping down to the water. Frequently, the relatively rare bobolink nests in these fields and other birds, including hawks and wild turkeys, use them as well. The float to the final bridge and take-out at MA 7A is barely 15 minutes. The take-out is just before the bridge on the right.

2
Deerfield River

Below Shelburne Falls to Greenfield

Put-in Point	Take-out Points	Approximate Distance	Approximate Trip Time	Condition of Water	Portages
Bardwell Ferry Road bridge	I-91 bridges	4 miles	1 $\frac{1}{2}$ hours	Riffles	None
Bardwell Ferry Road bridge	US 5– MA 10	10 $\frac{1}{4}$ miles	3–3 $\frac{1}{2}$ hours	Riffles, then mostly smooth	None

Timing is all-important when planning a canoeing trip on the Deerfield River in northwestern Massachusetts. The Deerfield is a river of many moods. At times it is a crashing, churning, terrifying waterway. And at other times, and in stretches only a few miles away from the whitewater, the river can be so sedate, so serene you'll wonder if the water is moving at all. If you catch the Deerfield between these two extremes, you will experience one of the easiest and yet most rewarding trips in southern New England. Do the 10$\frac{1}{4}$-mile segment described here after high water, but before the river drops to its summer level, and you will be treated to a delightful 3$\frac{1}{2}$-hour float that begins amid ledges and forests and ends in a farmland valley.

This trip starts at the Bardwell Ferry Road bridge below the town of Shelburne Falls and finishes beside the US 5–MA 10 bridge near Greenfield. Some whitewater canoeists run another section of the upper Deerfield above Charlemont, but that area—which includes the notorious Zoar Gap—is extremely dangerous, especially in springtime. Several lives have been lost there over the years. It is definitely not recommended, except for experts.

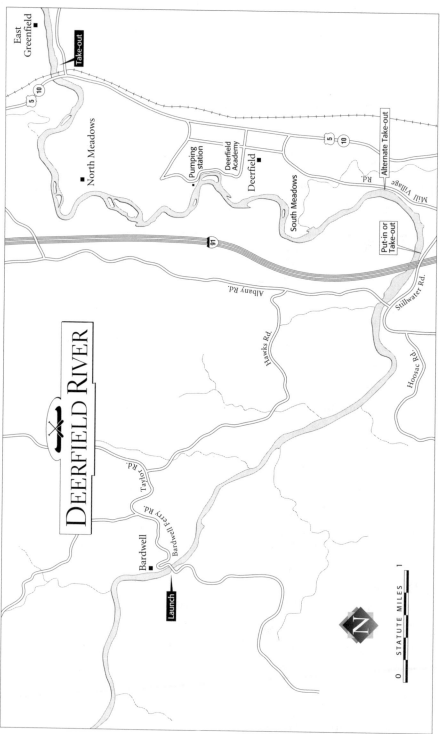

Deerfield River

East Greenfield

Take-out

North Meadows

Pumping station

Deerfield Academy

Deerfield

South Meadows

Mill Village Rd.

Alternate Take-out

Put-in or Take-out

91

Albany Rd.

Stillwater Rd.

Hoosac Rd.

Hawks Rd.

Taylor Rd.

Bardwell Ferry Rd.

Bardwell

Launch

N

0   STATUTE MILES   1

Although there are no dams on the section of the Deerfield described here, there are several upriver at Shelburne Falls that will affect your canoeing. The hilly terrain and the release of water at the dams can vary the flow considerably. The water level rises and drops quickly; to catch it at its best, go a few days after sudden thaws or heavy rains. We once canoed this stretch under ideal conditions—there was enough water so that we floated over rocks, had a steady current, and encountered no dangers. One week earlier, however, the river had been in flood stage.

Access

To leave a car at the take-out point, drive US 5–MA 10 to where it crosses the river just south of Greenfield. There is a small parking area on a side road on the south end of the bridge, just beyond a railroad bridge that parallels the highway bridge. Take-out here is not easy (up a steep, wooded slope), but paddling to this spot will provide your best taste of the Deerfield. A frequently used alternate take-out below the I-91 bridge is much easier, but leaving the water there makes for a short trip.

To haul your canoe to the put-in, follow US 5–MA 10 south to the sign indicating HISTORIC DEERFIELD on the right. Drive through this colonial-era village, past Deerfield Academy, and you will reach Mill Village Road, which takes you back to the river. (There is one small take-out on Mill Village Road, but it's so near I-91 that anybody desiring a short trip should use the I-91 take-out instead.) Turn right on Stillwater Road, pass under I-91, turn right onto Albany Road, and cross the river.

Now the driving adventure begins. One mile past the bridge, Hawks Road angles off to the left. Follow this narrow and winding hill road until it runs into Taylor Road in 2½ miles. Turn left onto Taylor Road and then left again at Bardwell Ferry Road. In another mile of switchback driving you'll arrive at the put-in. Park just beyond the high bridge. At the right rear corner of the parking area, which is often filled on weekends with the vehicles of fishermen, you'll find a path leading down to some large stones almost under the bridge. Launching here is easy. There are lots of riffles just upstream, but the river is usually relatively smooth beneath the bridge.

The River

This first stretch may be the prettiest of your trip. Certainly it provides the greatest feeling of wilderness. Ledges and rock outcroppings are scattered along both shores, alternating with stands of dense forest. Numerous little brooks cascade down the rocky slopes in early spring and after heavy rains. You may even get lucky—as we did—and spot a beaver swimming by. There are several colonies in the area, although the beavers usually remain in the smaller streams.

You will come to your first set of riffles quickly, but when there is enough water they are no problem. Nor are most of the others that have to be negotiated at brief intervals. In low water, the riffles are bottom-scrapers or worse. But if you go at the recommended time—when the river is slightly high—they are just fun. You will zoom right over the rocks in a fast current. Only a few spots are wild enough to be considered more than riffles, and they are no more than Class I rapids in the American Canoe Association rating system. The river is wide and pretty all the way, and as you progress there are more smooth stretches than riffly ones. Sandbars jut out from the shores and combine with boulders and ledges to provide many inviting spots for resting, fishing, or picture taking.

You should reach the Albany Road bridge in about an hour. The next set of bridges, the double I-91 crossings, is just a short distance farther, past one more lengthy riffle. If you elect to take out here, swing to the right under the second bridge. Beyond I-91 the river runs through farmland, passes through an area called South Meadows, swings around the town of Deerfield, and meanders through North Meadows on the way to your take-out. There are several shallow spots where the river runs around gravel bars in the first mile or so past I-91, but the current remains strong and finding the main channel is not difficult.

You will get only an occasional glimpse of buildings in Deerfield as you pass the village. You can tie up and walk into the town, however,

Picturesque riffles are just upstream from the Deerfield put-in.

when you reach a brick pumping station on your right. There is a road here, behind Deerfield Academy, but it is not a good alternate take-out because the slope is steep and covered with jagged stones. The remaining 3 miles from Deerfield to the US 5–MA 10 bridge are very smooth and relaxing. The river flows slightly deeper and divides around a string of islands. Although trees continue to line the banks, the setting is obviously pastoral. You may see herds of cattle drowsing in the shade or hear tractors being worked in the nearby fields. When you reach the Green River coming in from the left, itself a tranquil little stream here after tumultuous beginnings farther north, you are nearing the end of your trip.

The take-out point is easy to find. In addition to the highway and railroad bridges you float under, look for concrete pillars and stone abutments remaining from long-vanished structures. Pull out on the right, just beyond the railroad bridge.

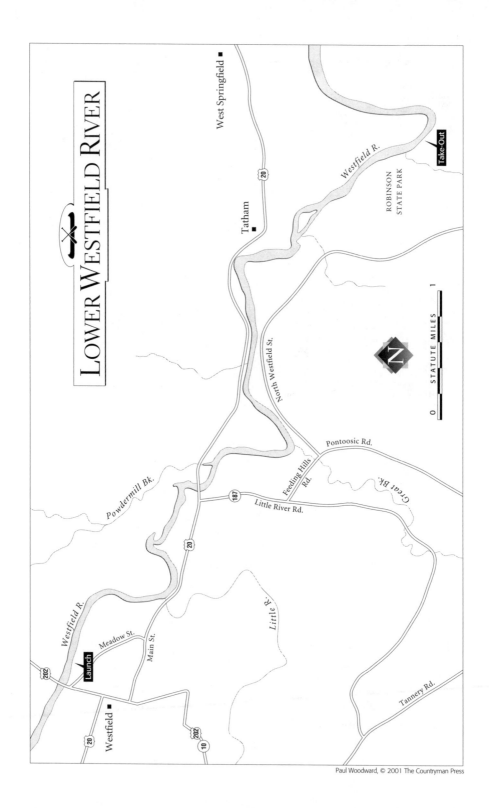

LOWER WESTFIELD RIVER

West Springfield

Tatham

Westfield R.

North Westfield St.

ROBINSON
STATE PARK

Take-Out

20

Pontoosic Rd.

Feeding Hills Rd.

Great Bk.

Powdermill Bk.

187

Little River Rd.

20

Little R.

Westfield R.

Meadow St.

Main St.

Launch

202

20

Westfield

202

10

Tannery Rd.

STATUTE MILES

0   1

N

3

Lower Westfield River

Westfield to West Springfield

Put-in Point	Take-out Point	Approximate Distance	Approximate Trip Time	Condition of Water	Portages
Meadow Street, Westfield	Robinson State Park	6¼ miles	2½–3 hours	Mostly smooth, frequent riffles	None

Serious canoeists throughout New England know the upper branches of the Westfield River in western Massachusetts; together the three branches form one of the longest and best whitewater streams in the region. The Westfield was designated an official Wild and Scenic River in 1993, and certainly deserves the recognition.

The lower Westfield, the stretch described here, is a different story. Very wide, it offers little challenge to whitewater canoeists, and some sections are less than wild and scenic, but it can provide a most pleasant few hours of paddling for those more interested in wildlife and leisurely floating than in roaring chutes and splashing thrills. Still, although this section is considered flatwater, it is not completely flat. Under normal water conditions, there are enough riffles interspersed with the smooth stretches to keep paddlers alert and give them a slight taste of what the more adventurous find upstream. This segment also has the advantage of being navigable most of the year; the three branches that tumble out of the western hills can usually be canoed only in early spring.

This trip begins at a launch spot in the town of Westfield and ends at John C. Robinson State Park, a big park in Agawam in West Springfield. It is possible to follow the Westfield River all the way to the Connecticut River, but that means adding a difficult portage around a dam in the state park. It might be better to terminate the trip in the park, at a take-out a short distance above the dam, and eliminate the last few miles.

Keep in mind that the park doesn't open until 10 AM, so you will be unable to leave a car at the take-out until that time. You can leave a vehicle outside the gate earlier, if you wish, and then walk up to it later, but that is a relatively long walk.

Access

The put-in at Westfield is at a marked launch site off Meadow Street, about 50 yards downstream from the MA10–US 202 bridge, easily accessible from I-90, the Massachusetts Turnpike. The launch is down a path from a parking area that also serves a popular river walkway.

To leave a car at Robinson State Park, follow Meadow Street east to Main Street (US 20), turn left, and follow Main until reaching Little River Road (MA 187). From here, follow signs that lead to the park. You will turn right onto Little River Road, then go left on Feeding Hills Road, and left on North Street to the park entrance. By road, the distance from the put-in to the park is about 7 miles. Once in the park, follow signs downhill to the take-out.

The take-out itself is easily missed from the water, so before leaving the take-out, follow the path to the water and look for landmarks. A stone abutment from a vanished bridge will be your signal; when you come downriver and see the abutment standing alone out in the water, it's time to look for the narrow take-out trail.

The River

Back at the put-in, swing out toward the left bank to catch the stronger current and the most ambiance. You may begin seeing wildlife, or at least signs, immediately because the left bank has numerous trails and dens of woodchucks, and there are many signs of beaver activity. We've also seen ducks and geese on this segment, along with kingfishers, swallows, sandpipers, and many songbirds.

As soon as you round the first bend you reach riffles, the first of

An ancient sycamore leans over the Westfield River.

many sets on this trip. Most are simply rocky strips that can be floated over, but a few require a little maneuvering. In general, the riffles in the first half of the trip are more frequent but easier, while those well downstream are farther between but have larger rocks and require a bit more care. In low water, paddlers may get hung up occasionally.

At first, you are paddling behind homes on the right shore, but then you find a highway, US 20, just above you on the right. The traffic noise is a bit intrusive, but the general attractiveness of the waterway offers some consolation. Throughout most of the trip the river is flanked by large trees, many of which lean out over the water.

As you approach the first bridge, probably in just under an hour, look over the high, steep bank on your left. Numerous holes in the soil show that this is the site of a bank swallow colony; if you pass by in early summer you should see numerous swallows going in and out of the tunnels. A few larger holes are the nesting tunnels of kingfishers. We've seen muskrats in this area, too, along with squirrels and more woodchucks.

The bridge is for US 20, and later you will have the highway on your left for a considerable distance. Beyond the bridge is an area where several pieces of junk and debris are strewn down the banks; cleaning this section would go a long way toward enhancing the pleasure of a float down the Westfield.

Even here, though, there is wildlife. Look closely at the trees and you are likely to see signs of beavers. The animals don't attempt to dam the Westfield—it is much too wide—and they don't build the classic stick-mound lodges. Instead, they tunnel into the banks, under the waterline, and could easily be overlooked if the gnawed trees didn't give them away.

When US 20 appears on the left shore, Robinson State Park begins on the right. Here, that shore is the more attractive. For the most part the river is smooth, but now the riffles that you do come to include larger rocks that require some dodging. Then, shortly after the river and the highway split, you reach a large island. Take the wider left passage even though entering it means negotiating a riffle.

Now you are in the final segment. The river is smooth enough for you to listen to orioles singing and to watch swallows darting over the water, with only a minor riffle or two remaining. You also are likely to see people enjoying the park, either walking a trail that runs near the river or simply lounging on the bank. When you see the stone abutment in the river, swing to the right. The take-out is shortly before the abutment, beside a little brook.

4
Quaboag River

Brookfield to Warren

Put-in Points	Take-out Point	Approximate Distance	Approximate Trip Time	Condition of Water	Portages
MA 148 bridge	Lucy Stone Park	6¾ miles	2½–3 hours	Smooth	None
MA 67 bridge	Lucy Stone Park	2½ miles	1 hour	Smooth	None

The Quaboag River in south-central Massachusetts is something of a "backward" river. Other rivers, particularly those in hilly country such as central and western Massachusetts, begin small and fast and eventually grow wider and slower. Not the Quaboag. This river is full grown at birth, a broad, languid stream meandering through marshland. Farther along, the Quaboag turns into a tumbling whitewater river.

Only experts should run the Quaboag rapids, which extend from Warren to Blanchardville, east of Springfield. But anyone who knows which end of a paddle to hold can do this trip on the upper Quaboag. Here the river is wide, smooth, and easy, with only the wind as a possible drawback. A strong breeze from the west or northwest can make you work hard in the first section of this trip, for the river is mostly open water with little protection from the elements. At all other times, canoeing the upper Quaboag is a most pleasant way for family groups or beginners to spend a few hours. The river wanders through a marsh rich in wildlife and aquatic plants, and then narrows somewhat as it enters woodlands. Finally, it picks up speed as it bubbles past a few minor riffles shortly before the take-out. The full distance of the trip is about 6¾ miles; it can usually be canoed in 2½ to 3 hours.

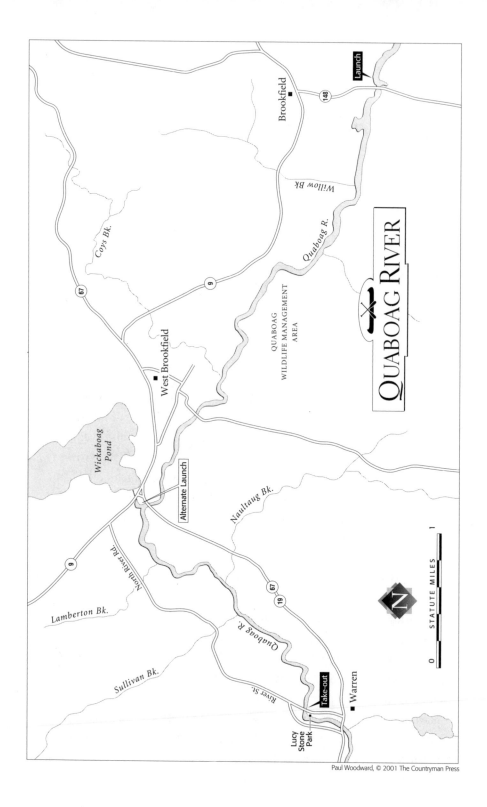

QUABOAG RIVER

Launch

Brookfield

148

Willow Bk.

Quaboag R.

Coys Bk.

67

9

QUABOAG
WILDLIFE MANAGEMENT
AREA

West Brookfield

Wickaboag
Pond

Alternate Launch

Naultaug Bk.

9

North River Rd.

Lamberton Bk.

67

19

Sullivan Bk.

Quaboag R.

River St.

Take-out

Warren

Lucy
Stone
Park

N

STATUTE MILES

0   1

Paul Woodward, © 2001 The Countryman Press

Access

The take-out is in Warren, at Lucy Stone Park, a small parking area be-side a bridge on River Street (called Old West Brookfield Road outside the village of Warren), just upriver from the main part of the town. The park is on the west side of the road, at the spot where the river bends and then plunges into the first set of rapids. For those not familiar with quickwater techniques, the preferred take-out is just before the bridge on the left bank. Pulling out here and carrying your canoe across the road to your car is easier and safer than trying to combat the swifter currents and rocks beyond the bridge.

To reach the put-in, return to Warren and take MA 67 north to MA 9, or drive north on Old West Brookfield Road, which changes into Old Warren Road, until it meets MA 9. You can put in here, where MA 67 crosses the river, at a spot popular with fishermen. If you launch here, however, the distance to the bridge at Lucy Stone Park is only about 2½ miles, perhaps 1 hour on the water. Therefore, it is better to continue on MA 9 east through West Brookfield to MA 148 in Brookfield. Turn right on MA 148 and drive to the river. You will find good access on the left, just before the bridge.

The River

The MA 148 access is just west of Quaboag Pond, which is fed by smaller streams and in turn forms the Quaboag River. Because of this pond, nearby Wickaboag Pond, and other large ponds in its watershed, the Quaboag usually has plenty of water and can easily be canoed most of the year. The current and depth vary far less than in most rivers.

The best time to begin this trip is usually early morning, before the wind springs up and while the wildlife is still active. You are likely to spot great blue herons prowling the shallow areas on both sides of the river, as well as green herons, ducks of several varieties, and maybe even bitterns or rails—shy, elusive birds seldom seen away from marshes and certainly not seen by canoeists shooting rapids. Muskrats can be found here too, and occasionally an early riser may glimpse a mink or an otter.

The smooth Quaboag flows through open, marshy areas.

Little can be seen of the towns on the right as you move downriver, for the buildings are screened by trees. On the left, a series of hills makes up the horizon. By the time you reach the first bridge at West Brookfield, the river is beginning to narrow slightly, but it retains its marshy atmosphere until just beyond the MA 67 bridge, approximately 4¼ miles from your start. Here the river curves to the left and for the first time flows close to the trees.

Very soon, though, you will leave the trees and return to paddling in an open marsh. As the forest falls away you will be presented with good views of the hillsides and some of the area's alluring old farms— weathered buildings, lush meadows, and miles of stone walls. Those rocky slopes may be hard to plow, but they are certainly appealing to the passerby.

This swampy section belongs to red-winged blackbirds and swallows, but the bird population changes as the river narrows and reenters the woods. Orioles, kingbirds, and vireos can be seen in the overhead branches, and warblers and wrens seem to follow along with you in the undergrowth on the shores. You should also see signs of beavers (such as gnawed trees and chewed-off branches), which have moved into the area in recent years.

Look for a brook that adds to the current joining the river from the right. Soon you will see a few boulders scattered about. There are no rapids, but occasionally you will encounter brief riffles, all easy to handle. The Quaboag is a forest river now, with tall birches, maples, and oaks, high banks complete with muskrat and otter slides, and a steady current. Little effort beyond steering around the numerous bends is required in this area.

When you come abreast of several large boulders on a point reaching out from the left, you are nearing your trip's end. Just beyond the point, the River Street–Old West Brookfield Road bridge comes into view. Swing to the left shore and take out before reaching the bridge. If you go under the bridge you might get a taste of the "other" Quaboag—tumbling whitewater—whether you want to or not.

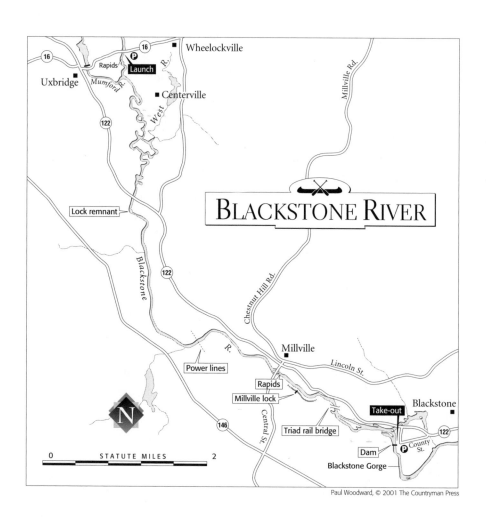

Uxbridge

Wheelockville

16

16

Rapids
Launch

Mumford R.

Centerville

West R.

Millville Rd.

122

Lock remnant

BLACKSTONE RIVER

Blackstone

122

Chestnut Hill Rd.

Millville

R.

Power lines

Lincoln St.

Rapids

Millville lock

Blackstone

N

146

Central St.

Triad rail bridge

Take-out

122

Dam

County St.

0   STATUTE MILES   2

Blackstone Gorge

5
Blackstone River

Uxbridge to Blackstone

Put-in Point	Take-out Point	Approximate Distance	Approximate Trip Time	Condition of Water	Portages
MA 16, Uxbridge	Blackstone Gorge	7½ miles	3½ hours	Mostly smooth, some riffles	None

This section of the Blackstone River, running from the mill village of Uxbridge to a gorgeous gorge at the Rhode Island line, offers a good look back at the stonework of another era. At many points along this trip you can see the remains of mills, canals, and locks left over from the early 19th century, when the Blackstone was considered "the hardest working river in the country."

Today, canoeing down this river is a quiet, peaceful experience. Most of the trip is flatwater but with a steady current until you near the take-out. There are sections of riffles, depending upon the water level, and one short but significant stretch of rapids that might require lining through or carrying around. Usually, though, there are no portages, and the entire 7½ miles is a quick and easy run with plenty of time for looking around.

And you should take your time on this trip. Plan on stopping below Millville (site of the brief rapids) to examine the Millville Lock, one of the best remaining examples of the stone locks that once operated the famed Blackstone Canal that ferried freight between Worcester and Providence and helped usher in America's industrial age. Also, you will float under the Triad Bridge, an ambitious project in which three railroad tracks were to cross the river at the same spot, using three different

The dam signals the completion of your Blackstone float.

levels. The top level was never completed, but its stone pillars remain towering above the water.

Still more time should be spent, before or after your trip, walking along the Blackstone Gorge just below your take-out. On the Rhode Island side of the state line, this gorge is simply beautiful, and trails can lead you to high outcroppings far above the scene or down to spots very close to the tumbling, roaring rapids.

Access

To leave a car at the take-out, drive MA 122 into the village of Blackstone. Near the Rhode Island line look for County Road and a sign for the Blackstone Gorge. Follow County Road and the signs to the river and a small parking area. The dam is just ahead, and the gorge on your left.

Reaching the put-in is a simple matter. Return to MA 122 and go north (left). In 2½ miles you reach the center of Millville. At Central Street, turn left for a look at the river; the rapids are directly below the bridge. Because the river divides around an island as it approaches the bridge, you'll have to decide which side to paddle. The right passage (as you face downstream) is usually less intimidating, normally Class I or II rapids. The left channel is more intimidating or challenging—depending on your perspective—often Class II or III. After looking over these rapids, return to MA 122 and continue going north until reaching MA 16 in downtown Uxbridge. Turn right on MA 16, cross the first river (Mumford River), and continue to the edge of the village, where you cross the Blackstone River bridge. A dirt lane just beyond the bridge on the right leads to your put-in.

The River

At the put-in are riffles from a mass of stone blocks. If you are the adventurous sort you can put in above them and immediately get a taste of quickwater. Or you can easily put in below them and begin with flatwater.

Much of the first part of this trip includes floating over minor riffles and steering around small islands. There are no buildings in this stretch and you soon may forget you are in a long-industrialized part of the state. Tall trees line the river, including stately sycamores, many of which are old and full of character. The river curves often and you have to be aware of blowdowns; however, the river is wide enough so that you should have no trouble paddling around the fallen trees.

Early in the trip the Mumford River enters from the right, and before you reach the first bridge the small West River joins from the left. The first bridge is a railroad span, and soon after you will float under MA 122. Now, look on your right to a low ridge running along the river; this is the old towpath for the canal. If you pull out in this segment you can see what is left of the canal a short distance in the woods. Here it resembles a sunken roadway. Better views of it are ahead.

You will pass stone abutments of a long-vanished bridge, and a few hundred yards beyond that, if you look carefully on your right, you can find some of the stonework of a lock built where the canal rejoined the river. This stonework is interesting, but the Millville Lock ahead is a better example of how the locks were built.

The river now is wider and smoother, with fewer curves and islands. A few homes are visible on the left, and later you will see buildings and hear the traffic on a road above on the right. When more
homes appear high above on the left, you are nearing Millville. Two immense boulders in the river indicate you are approaching the island for
the Central Street bridge. It's time to decide which channel to take.

The island itself was the site of several mills over the years, going
back to 1732, but if you are canoeing by it you'll have little time to look
around. The current increases greatly here. If you are not willing to try
running the rapids, it is possible to take out on the left side of the right
channel, carry across the island beneath the bridge, and relaunch, but
that is not an easy portage. When the water level is very low, you might
have to line your canoe over some of the largest rocks just beyond the
bridge.

Much stonework from early structures remains around the bridge
and along the next stretch of river. As you resume floating downstream,
keep an eye on the right shore. About half a mile or less from the rapids
you reach an opening in the trees, where a tiny brook empties into the
river. Pull out here. The big Millville Lock is a short distance in the
woods. Built in 1828 of huge stone blocks, it is some 30 yards long and
about 12 feet high and is considered the best-preserved lock on the entire Blackstone Canal.

Below the lock you float under a railroad bridge and then swing
very close to MA 122 briefly before rounding a bend and reaching the
Triad Bridge. The first two tiers of the bridge are metal, but just beyond,
look for the high cement abutments on each side of the river that were
to hold the third tier. In summer, these pillars may be hard to find because trees now are crowding in on them. Much smaller abutments in
the river itself will tell you just where to look.

The remainder of your trip is an easy float on quiet water down to
your take-out at the dam. You are likely to hear the water pouring down
into the gorge before seeing the DANGER sign on the stone ends of the
dam. Pull out on the left. Then take a walk along the gorgeous gorge.

6

Concord River

Concord to Billerica

Put-in Point	Take-out Points	Approximate Distance	Approximate Trip Time	Condition of Water	Portages
Lowell Road access	MA 225 bridge	4$^{1}/_{4}$ miles	2 hours	Smooth	None
Lowell Road access	River Street bridge	8$^{1}/_{2}$ miles	4–4$^{1}/_{2}$ hours	Smooth	None
Lowell Road access	MA 3A bridge	10 miles	4$^{1}/_{2}$–5 hours	Smooth	None

> *I have often stood on the banks of the Concord, watching the lapse of the current, an emblem of all progress, following the same law with the system, with time, and all that is made; the weeds at the bottom gently bending down the stream, shaken by the watery wind, still planted where their seeds had sunk, but ere long to die and go down likewise; the shining pebbles, not yet anxious to better their condition, the chips and weeds, and occasional logs and stems of trees that floated past, fulfilling their fate, were objects of singular interest to me, and at last I resolved to launch myself on its bosom, and float whither it would bear me.*

So wrote Henry David Thoreau in 1839 in his book *A Week on the Concord and Merrimack Rivers.* While launching yourself on the Concord today and floating whither it bears you may not inspire the poetry and philosophy that it did for Thoreau, the river remains

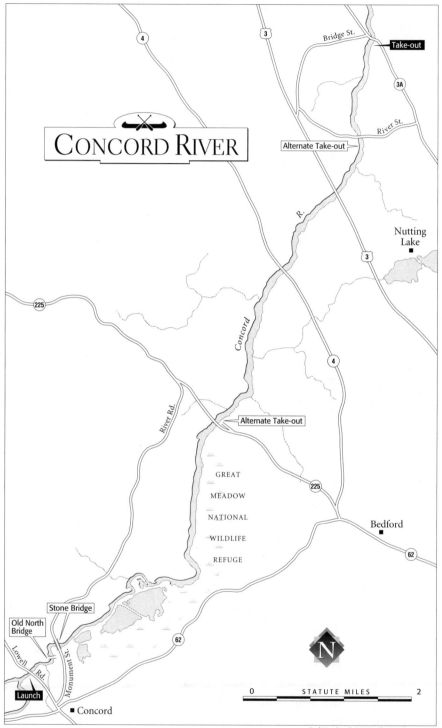

CONCORD RIVER

Take-out

Alternate Take-out

Bridge St.

River St.

Nutting Lake

Alternate Take-out

Concord

Concord R.

River Rd.

GREAT

MEADOW

NATIONAL

WILDLIFE

REFUGE

Stone Bridge

Old North Bridge

Lowell Rd.

Monument St.

Launch

Concord

Bedford

N

0   STATUTE MILES   2

Paul Woodward, © 2001 The Countryman Press

among the best waterways in northeastern Massachusetts for relaxed canoe touring. From Concord to Billerica, you will find 10 miles of smooth water with no portages, plenty of attractive shoreline scenery, and a great deal of history.

Early in your trip you will pass beneath a replica of the Old North Bridge, where the first shots of the Revolutionary War were fired. The hillsides of this area, now silent and serene, rang out in 1775 with the call to arms of the "embattled farmers." It takes only a little knowledge of those events to make a cruise down the Concord River something special.

I recommend making this trip in autumn rather than summer, for the Concord is often crowded with powerboats during the warmer months, particularly on weekends. Moreover, in autumn you will reap the full benefit of the foliage, and get to enjoy the ducks and geese that flock to a wildlife refuge that flanks a long section of your journey. Also, you will be more closely following Thoreau's adventure, for he made his trip by rowboat in September.

Access

This trip can be shortened very easily, with excellent access for take-outs available at the MA 225 bridge (about $4\frac{1}{4}$ miles from Concord), or at River Street in Billerica ($8\frac{1}{2}$ miles). For the full 10 miles, however, leave a car next to the bridge on MA 3A north of Billerica. Then, to haul your canoe to the put-in, drive south 5 miles on Concord Road to MA 62, turn right and continue all the way to Concord, about 10 miles. By the Colonial Inn, turn right onto Lowell Road and travel just beyond the village to the river. A public access lane is on the left, just before the bridge.

The River

Just minutes after launching at the Lowell Road bridge, you will reach the site of the historic skirmish of April 19, 1775. A wooden bridge, built on the order of the original, arches over the water. Often this bridge is crowded with tourists, for it is located in the Minute Man

National Historic Park. Float under the bridge and then pull out on the right for a brief stroll. It is worth the time and effort. You will find markers commemorating the British soldiers who fell that day on the right side of the river. Cross the bridge for a look at the Minute Man statue and its inscription from the famous Emerson poem:

> *By the rude bridge that arched the flood,*
> *Their flag to April's breeze unfurled,*
> *Here once the embattled farmers stood,*
> *And fired the shot heard round the world.*
> *(from "Hymn Sung at the Completion of the Battle*
> *Monument, Concord, Massachusetts")*

Back on the river, you soon come to another picturesque bridge, this one made of stone. From this point it is calm and peaceful paddling for some distance between wooded banks, with silver maples the dominant trees. You quickly enter the sprawling Great Meadows National Wildlife Refuge; signs indicating such are on both sides of the river. Some of the signs show that areas of the refuge are closed to the public, but after half an hour or so of paddling you reach an open lane and a bench on the right. You can pull out here and go inland for a walk on the lanes that run around the marshes, where waterfowl congregate in autumn. Often you will hear far more geese and ducks than you can see, the gabbling, a true song of fall, accompanying you for several miles down the river. At times, though, the birds' calls may be drowned out by the planes from nearby Hanscom Field.

Soon you will leave the tall trees and high banks behind and move into an open, swampy area where the river widens and bushes are the primary vegetation. Even though still in the refuge, you will now be able to see numerous fine homes guarded by stately groves of pines on the hills to the left and a few on the right.

At the next bridge, MA 225, there is a public landing site on the right. Boating activity in this area and over the next few miles can be heavy. The river is open and easy from here for the 2 miles to the MA 4 bridge (poor access), where the wildlife refuge ends. The stretch of the

A replica of the Old North Bridge delights Concord paddlers.

river just beyond MA 4 passes numerous homes, most of which are equipped with boats, ramps, piers, and little beaches. After this segment the river narrows and becomes more attractive as you pass the double bridges for US 3 (no access). Oaks and maples, resplendent in autumn, crowd the banks, and you are likely to flush herons and sandpipers, as well as ducks, as you paddle around the bends.

It takes about an hour to complete the trip from the US 3 bridges, past the nearby River Street bridge, where a take-out is possible on the left, to your planned terminus just before the MA 3A bridge. Houses line this last stretch on the left side, and then you will see the businesses on MA 3A. A number of restaurants emphasize your return to the present. Thoreau also ended his first day's journey near here, but he dined that night on wild huckleberries.

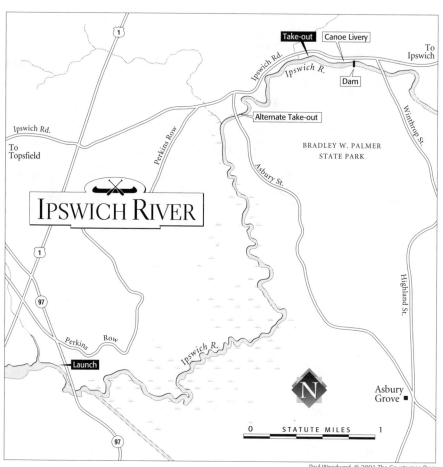

Ipswich Rd.

1

Take-out
Canoe Livery

To
Ipswich

Ipswich Rd.

Ipswich R.

Dam

Winthrop St.

Ipswich Rd.

To
Topsfield

Perkins Row

Alternate Take-out

BRADLEY W. PALMER
STATE PARK

Asbury St.

IPSWICH RIVER

1

97

Perkins Row

Highland St.

Ipswich R.

Launch

N

Asbury
Grove

0   STATUTE MILES   1

97

Paul Woodward, © 2001 The Countryman Press

7
Ipswich River

Topsfield to Ipswich Road

Put-in Point	Take-out Points	Approximate Distance	Approximate Trip Time	Condition of Water	Portages
MA 97 bridge	Asbury Street bridge	6 miles	2½–3 hours	Smooth	None
MA 97 bridge	Ipswich Road	7 miles	3–3½ hours	Smooth	None

One of the more popular canoeing rivers in eastern Massachusetts, the Ipswich is like a fine wine or a good book. It should never be hurried through, but tasted and savored a little bit at a time. Pause often and absorb the atmosphere. It can be most rewarding.

The stretch described here runs through Wenham Swamp southeast of Topsfield. This is the most intriguing portion of the river, and the part most easily canoed at any time of the year. During high-water periods you can continue all the way downriver into the village of Ipswich. The last several miles, however, are impassable during much of the summer and autumn. This lower section also includes two portages and stretches of fast water.

From the MA 97 (Salem Road) bridge to Ipswich Road, however, you'll have no portages and all smooth water. The total distance, snaking through the vast swamp, is approximately 7 miles, although you can shorten the trip slightly by taking out at the Asbury Street bridge. Canoeing at a leisurely pace, the paddle to Asbury Street takes only about 3 hours, and it's just a few minutes more to Ipswich Road.

Unlike many swamps, which resemble weedy millponds, Wenham

Swamp is liberally sprinkled with vibrant stands of trees, many perched on attractive islands and knolls. Even when you're out in the most open parts of the swamp, you'll never be far from a wooded retreat. The fascination of swamp life, however, is there. Make this trip in summer or early autumn, and you'll be accompanied by herons, bitterns, egrets, and sandpipers, the long-legged, long-billed birds that haunt such places. Most of the swamp is a wildlife sanctuary and therefore protected.

Access

In summertime, the current is usually so slow you can canoe upriver if you wish. Many people who use this river do just that, renting canoes from a livery on Ipswich Road, going upriver into the swamp, and floating back down. You can do the same thing by driving along Ipswich Road just east of the village of Topsfield and putting in from one of the several access spots above the dam where the river runs parallel to the road.

For a one-way trip, however, leave a car here or beside the bridge on nearby Asbury Street and then head west in another car. Turn left (south) on US 1 and follow it to MA 97 (Salem Road). A left turn here and a short drive bring you to the river. A canoe launch spot, so marked, is on the right shoulder before the bridge.

The River

After launching into the feeder stream, go to the left and you'll quickly be in the river at the bridge. In low water it might be a bit scratchy going under the bridge, but you should stay afloat if you paddle down the middle of the river. Very quickly you will pass beneath a railroad bridge and then see a wide and straight canal angling off to the right. As tempting as the canal might be, it won't take you to your car. Instead, take the shallow left fork, the regular river channel. In this early stretch, the canal may seem even more attractive because frequently there are snags and blowdowns in the river, but in a matter of minutes you'll be in deeper water and moving smoothly.

Egrets are among the many birds likely to be seen by Ipswich paddlers.

The river remains narrow as it winds its way between rocks and sandbars, flanked by willows and silver maples. Within half an hour of your start you will swing around a bend and pass a pine-crowned ridge on the right with a sign that identifies it as Perkins Island. Camping is permitted here only by reservation made through the Massachusetts Audubon Society. However, you may land and walk about. This is one of many such resting spots along the river. You may see groups of people with binoculars along the left shore. Footpaths in this area are used extensively by bird-watchers checking out a marsh hidden from canoeists. For the next mile or so, you'll have very pleasant paddling between forested shores. Oaks compete with maples for attention, and grapevines swarm over the lower bushes. You will also pass another small camping area, Colt Island, where overnight stays are by permission only.

When you leave the woods behind and move out into the more open parts of the swamp, the river meanders back and forth in a series of hairpin turns. During the summer months, tall marsh plants crowd the shoreline and limit your horizons. Colorful wildflowers, however, produce more than adequate compensation. In late summer and early autumn, a lavender plant called purple loosestrife is particularly enchanting. These "weedy" areas are the favorite feeding grounds of the gangling, 4-foot-tall great blue herons. Often you can follow one for a considerable distance down the river as it flees just one curve at a time ahead of your canoe. Songbirds such as kingbirds, warblers, flycatchers, and orioles abound here as well.

Occasionally, shortcut channels will enable you to lop off some of the half circles, and from time to time you will return to woods briefly before breaking out into the open again. There are only a few homes visible from the river. When you pass an impressive estate high on a hill on the right, however, you'll be within 1/2 mile or so of the Asbury Street bridge. You will also pass under a private wooden horse bridge belonging to the estate.

About 20 or 30 minutes more of paddling around sharp turns brings you to Asbury Street. The bridge here is known locally as Palmer Bridge, for it is nearly at the front gate of Bradley W. Palmer State Park (no camping), which reaches down to the right shore of the river just beyond the bridge. If you are ending your trip here, the best take-out is on the left side just beyond the bridge.

If you are continuing along the last leg toward the canoe livery or the Ipswich Road take-outs, just keep paddling. This final short stretch is possibly the most attractive of all, with majestic trees on both sides of the river. In fact, even if you left your car at Asbury Street, this segment is so pretty it is worth canoeing down toward the dam and back just to enjoy the surroundings.

8

Charles River

Medfield to South Natick

Put-in Point	Take-out Point	Approximate Distance	Approximate Trip Time	Condition of Water	Portages
West Street bridge	Pleasant Street Picnic Area	9 miles	3½–4 hours	Smooth	None

No canoeing guide for southern New England would be complete without a trip on the famed Charles River. The Charles has been a major transportation waterway since the founding of Boston, and in earlier centuries was the American Indians' connecting link between the sea and inland Massachusetts. Yet, for all its popularity as a "city river," it passes through long stretches of peaceful country. And just a few miles upriver from where sailboats and racing sculls crowd each other, you can enjoy tranquil day trips paddling through lush lowlands and woodlands.

The Charles winds some 85 miles on its way to Boston Harbor. Most of it is canoeable, at least in spring, but the most attractive stretch is this 9-mile section between the West Street bridge in Medfield and the dam at South Natick. This is a trip well within the limits of novices and family groups, for there are no rapids or portages, and the current is smooth and moderate. Along the way you will travel through marshy meadows and past towering rock ledges, and float between shorelines decorated with imposing stands of maples, hemlocks, birches, and oaks.

This trip of approximately 4 hours features manufactured attractions as well as natural delights. You will paddle under old train trestles and pass many elegant homes, the intriguing Death Bridge, then a statue perched on a ledge overlooking the river, and finally an elaborate footbridge before reaching your destination at South Natick.

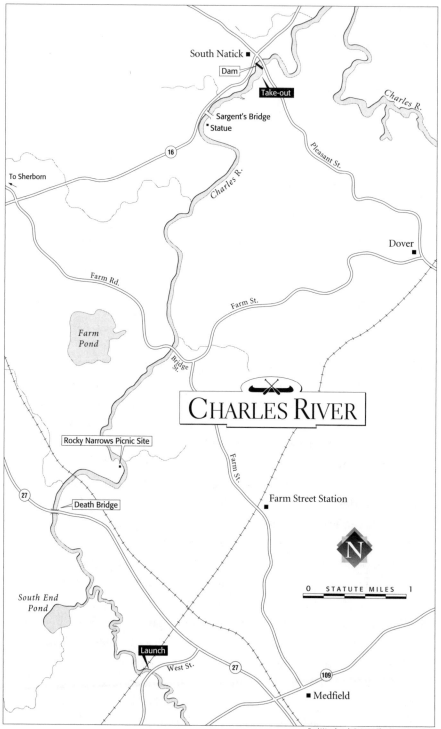

South Natick ■

Dam

Take-out

Charles R.

Sargent's Bridge
■ Statue

16

Pleasant St.

To Sherborn

Charles R.

Dover ■

Farm Rd.

Farm St.

Farm
Pond

Bridge St.

CHARLES RIVER

Rocky Narrows Picnic Site

Farm St.

27

Death Bridge

Farm Street Station ■

N

0   STATUTE MILES   1

South End
Pond

Launch

West St.

27

109

■ Medfield

Paul Woodward, © 2001 The Countryman Press

Access

To leave a car at the take-out, drive on MA 16 into South Natick. At Pleasant Street, turn east, crossing the river just below the dam. Your take-out will be through a small picnic area on the river's shore. There is parking space for several cars along the street.

After leaving a car, you can reach the recommended launching site by driving MA 16 southwest to MA 27, turning left, and following MA 27 into Medfield. Turn right at a traffic light onto West Street (before reaching Medfield village) and drive ½ mile to a bridge. Just before the bridge, take a short road to the right that runs between the highway and a railroad bed. It provides an excellent put-in beneath the bridge.

The River

Almost immediately you will paddle under a railroad crossing set on wooden pilings and pass through a small wooded area. Then you will reach an open marshland that dominates this segment of the Charles. The river snakes its way back and forth through a generally treeless plain for most of the way to the next bridge. Painted turtles and bullfrogs, soaking up the sunshine, are abundant along the shores here in summer, and red-winged blackbirds that live in the tall marsh grasses keep up a spirited and raucous protest, particularly during nesting time. In autumn, when the frogs and turtles are gone, migrating ducks can often be found feeding and resting in these marsh meadows.

It can be a long paddle through the marsh, and some canoeists make it longer by mistakenly veering off into a side channel that runs to a large pond. Some care must be taken to stay with the current around the sharp bends. If you reach a big pond, you have to backtrack.

The next landmark is the ominous-sounding Death Bridge. Earlier, when you drove MA 27 from the take-out in South Natick, you crossed this bridge, a modern structure that replaced an earlier bridge. Formerly, a sign with the Death Bridge name was displayed for passing motorists but is no longer in place. Legends have sprung up around the name, most of them dealing with grisly murders or tragic suicides. But the origin is far less dramatic. The bridge was named for a family—the

Marshy segments of the Charles hold birds such as red-winged blackbirds.

Death family—that once lived nearby. The family eventually tired of problems with its name and changed it to Derth. The old name remains on the bridge, although without the sign the sense of foreboding that used to touch those who paddled beneath it is missing.

Just minutes beyond Death Bridge you will find another railroad trestle, this one of rusty steel. Then, moments later, you will arrive at one of the highlights of the trip, a rocky bluff on the left shore. The opportunity to take a break here and climb the bluff is almost irresistible, especially on sizzling summer days when the open marsh meadows can become virtual frying pans. (It is possible to put in at Death Bridge and skip the first few miles of this trip, but launching and parking are much more convenient at the West Street bridge.) There are a few scraggly trees clinging to the ledges—enough for some shade. Some canoeists tote their picnic fixings with them when they climb the bluff. It's a most scenic spot for a leisurely rest.

Beyond the bluff the river makes a sweeping turn, almost a half circle, around to the left. It then carries you through perhaps the best-known area of this stretch, the picturesque Rocky Narrows. Here hemlock-cloaked bluffs crowd the river on both sides, although the water is still smooth and not particularly narrow. Just beyond the narrowest passage, on the left, is an official picnic spot, a clearing with a sign that welcomes canoeists. It is part of the Rocky Narrows Reservation, administered by the Trustees of Reservations.

After this you will continue to pass through delightful woodlands punctuated with glimpses of a few stately homes in the distance. Then, about 20 minutes after paddling through Rocky Narrows, you will come to a low, concrete bridge at Farm Road in Sherborn. Farm Road roughly follows the route of a famous Indian trail, the Connecticut Path. Just beyond the bridge you will pass a second public area, called the Peters Reservation, in a pine grove on the right.

Then, for a long stretch, you paddle and float through pleasant forest. You may see a trail marked with blue and yellow blazes on the left shore. This area is part of the Broadmoor Wildlife Sanctuary of the Massachusetts Audubon Society. Eventually, you pass a string of homes of varying sizes and designs on the right. Fortunately, they do little to detract from the aesthetic value of the river. The water here is very shallow, with a rocky bottom, but paddling through remains easy in all but the driest of seasons.

As you near South Natick there are more houses and a road (MA 16) on the left, but what catches your eye is the statue on the right. Standing just a few feet above the river on a huge boulder, the figure of a young woman in prayerful pose watches over the water. Just beyond is the elaborate, triple-arched wooden footbridge known locally as Sargent's Bridge. Myths surround this area, too. Some townspeople say the statue commemorates a child who drowned near here. According to a South Natick historian, however, both the statue and the bridge were erected by Daniel Sargent, who owned a huge estate on the left side of the river and a farm on the right side. Wanting to preserve the beauty of the shoreline, he planted rhododendrons and other flowering trees, then added the statue as a finishing touch.

After floating by several more homes on the left, you will reach the deadwater from the dam. Paddle to the right side of the dam to your take-out at the small picnic area.

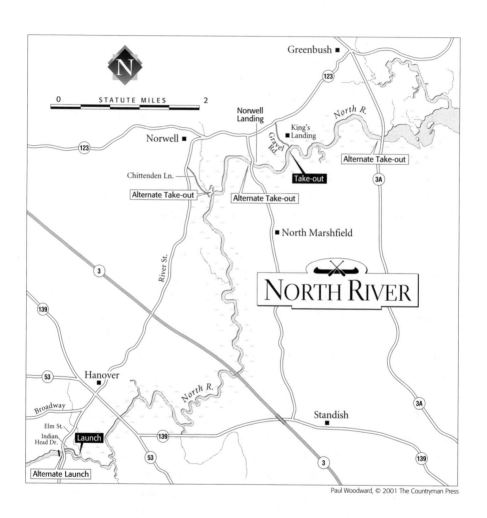

STATUTE MILES

Greenbush ■

123

North R.

Norwell
Landing

King's
■ Landing

Norwell ■

Gravel Rd.

Alternate Take-out

3A

Chittenden Ln.

Take-out

Alternate Take-out

Alternate Take-out

North Marshfield ■

River St.

NORTH RIVER

3

139

North R.

Hanover ■

53

Broadway

3A

Standish
■

Elm St.

Indian Head Dr.

Launch

139

Alternate Launch

53

3

139

9

North River

Hanover to Norwell

Put-in Point	Take-out Points	Approximate Distance	Approximate Trip Time	Condition of Water	Portages
Indian Head Drive	Chittenden Lane	7½ miles	2½–3 hours	Smooth (tidal)	None
Indian Head Drive	Bridge Street	8 miles	3 hours	Smooth (tidal)	None
Indian Head Drive	King's Landing	9 miles	3–3½ hours	Smooth (tidal)	None

The word *scenic* can be applied legitimately to many rivers in southern New England, including most of those found in this book, but for the North River the term is not only proper but official. The North, a tidal river a short distance south of Boston, was among the first chosen for protection under the Massachusetts Scenic Rivers Act. It deserves the honor.

The North River, which derives its name from a sister waterway called the South River that it joins where they together empty into the sea, is rich in history as well as physical attractions. Numerous shipyards crowded its banks from the late 17th century until after the Civil War. And for hundreds of years before that, Indian tribes used the North as a primary passage from the sea to inland Massachusetts and beyond. In fact, the North marks the start of the Wampanoag Commemorative Canoe Passage, a 50-mile river route used by the Wampanoag Indians to connect Massachusetts Bay with Narragansett Bay. Most of the shipyards are gone now, and fiberglass and aluminum canoes have replaced the birch-bark craft of the Indians, but the inexorable tides still surge in and out each day, making the North River a pleasant and interesting canoeing experience.

Access

Those planning to travel on the North have several options regarding trip distances. For one, the tides make this one of the easiest rivers on which to float both ways (be sure to check tide charts before starting out). Also, take-out points have been improved greatly in recent years. The last bridge before the river reaches the sea is MA 3A, but at that point the North is very wide and often crowded with powerboats. You can land at a marina by the MA 3A bridge, but there is a fee for the privilege. The next bridge upriver, on Bridge Street, has two good take-outs, but remember that the one on the north side of the river is for Norwell residents only. There is a good public launch on the southern side, built by a Marshfield conservation organization. You can leave a car here for a trip of about 8 miles and 3 hours.

For a slightly longer journey, and a chance to see some of the best scenery along the river, look for a place called King's Landing at the end of a long gravel road running off MA 123, about ½ mile east of Bridge Street, in Norwell. Canoes are available for rent at King's Landing, making it easy to launch there, go upriver, and return without hauling any gear at all. If you park here for take-out only, there is a small fee.

If a shorter, one-way trip sounds good, you can take out at Chittenden Lane, about 1½ miles upriver from King's Landing. This town-owned site with a small wooden dock lies at the end of a narrow street, both sides of which are private property, so parking space is limited to a car or two. Both the Bridge Street and King's Landing sites are better.

Whether using King's Landing or Bridge Street as your take-out, you can reach the put-in in Hanover by driving MA 123 west until a fork just west of Bridge Street. Take the left fork, Dover Street, which soon ends at River Street. Follow River Street southwest (quickly passing Chittenden Lane) until you cross MA 53–MA 139 in Hanover, where River Street becomes Broadway. In a short distance, Elm Street branches to the left off Broadway. Follow Elm Street to the river and

At the launch site, the North River is narrow and shady.

turn left onto Indian Head Drive just before reaching the bridge. A parking area and launch site are just ahead.

The River

The North almost immediately widens into the meandering marshland river that typifies its remaining miles. Low bushes and tall aquatic plants line both shores. Many of the plants add color during their blossoming periods, the blue and yellow wild irises being particularly eye catching. Tall trees form the background. Swallows and other birds add to the enchanting setting.

After about 30 minutes of paddling, you'll pass several elegant homes on the left just before reaching the MA 53–MA 139 bridge. Here you will begin feeling the effects of the tide. If your timing is right you will have an easy float. If the tide is still coming in, however, you will have to work.

Moments after passing the first bridge, you will paddle under a stone bridge at Washington Street, where there is a brief flurry of quickwater, and then return to the open marshes. The river wanders back and forth over the 3 miles from Washington Street to the next set of bridges, the double span for MA 3. In this stretch during the summer you may see powerboats, some towing skiers. It is best to stay near the shore to avoid the boats speeding around blind bends, although the river is wide enough for both boats and canoes. In this area, also, are the first of many signs along the left bank identifying sites of vanished shipyards.

Beyond MA 3, the river, while still wide and open, becomes more interesting, with several curves that take you near wooded knolls and hillsides on the right. These make fine picnic sites. Eventually, the river swings nearer trees and houses on the left, and you will pass more shipyard site signs. If you are taking out at Chittenden Lane, begin looking for the wooden dock on the left.

If taking out at Bridge Street, head for the right shore as you paddle through the widening expanse near the bridge. The take-out is in a grove of trees just before you reach the bridge.

If you are going on to King's Landing, extra care is necessary when passing beneath the Bridge Street bridge for two reasons—the strong current under the bridge and the usual flurry of activity at the Norwell town landing just beyond the bridge on the left. The final leg of your trip to King's Landing is through an extremely attractive stretch that features a marshland on the left shore and a forest on the right. It may be this section, perhaps more than any other, that qualifies the North as an official scenic river.

10

Nemasket River

Middleborough to North Middleborough

Put-in Point	Take-out Point	Approximate Distance	Approximate Trip Time	Condition of Water	Portages
Oliver Mill Park	Titicut Street bridge	5 ³/₄ miles	2 ¹/₂–3 hours	Smooth	None

The Nemasket River, east of the city of Taunton in southeastern Massachusetts, has become increasingly popular with canoeists and kayakers. There are good reasons. The segment described here begins at one of the most interesting and picturesque parks in the area; flows through a woodsy, swampy area with abundant wildlife; passes beneath an ancient stone bridge; then meanders considerably before emptying into the much larger Taunton River.

It is possible to take out before reaching the Taunton, at the Murdock Street bridge, but that would make for a trip of less than 3 miles and would prevent experiencing the differences between the winding Nemasket and the broad Taunton. Instead, it is better to paddle the Nemasket to its end, then go a mile or so on the Taunton and take out at the first bridge, Titicut Street, or even combine this trip with the Taunton River float (Trip 11).

The Nemasket usually has fairly good current, but there are no rapids or even riffles to be concerned with, so it is a trip suitable for families and beginners. Under usual water conditions there are no portages, although in high water or very low water the extremely low stone bridge might require a short carry. For the most part, it is a river that is ideal for leisurely floating and enjoying the scenery and bird life.

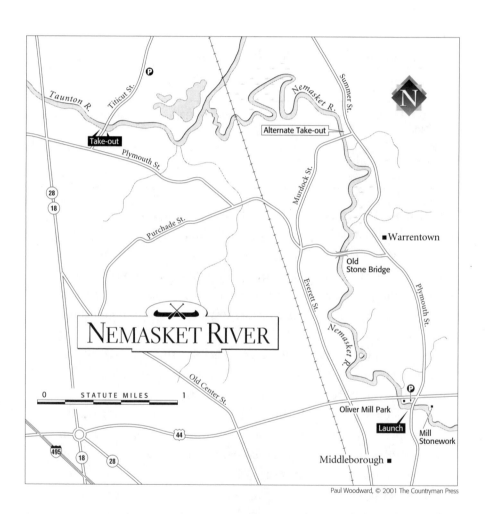

Paul Woodward, © 2001 The Countryman Press

Access

Put-in is at Middleborough's Oliver Mill Park on US 44 about $2\frac{1}{2}$ miles east of I-495. Before launching, spend some time looking over the stonework remaining from the colonial-era mill complex built by Peter Oliver. Footbridges enable visitors to cross the many channels and raceways that once served the complex. The largest channel now serves as a fish ladder that enables river herring and other fish to go upstream to spawn. The put-in is through the picnic area to the right of the stonework, where the herring channel rejoins the river.

To leave a car at the take-out, go west on US 44, cross the river, then take the first road to the right. This is Everett Street, which soon ends at Plymouth Street. Here, you can take Plymouth Street a short distance to the right for a look at the low stone bridge you'll have to pass under. Then turn around and follow Plymouth Street north. Murdock Street breaks off to the right and provides another look at the river. This bridge is an alternative take-out. You can park just beyond the bridge on the left. If planning to add the short segment on the Taunton, follow Plymouth Street as it turns west and continue until reaching Titicut Street. You'll be taking out on the near side of the river, but guardrails here mean you have to park several hundred feet beyond the bridge, on the right.

The River

Immediately after launching you glide around a bend and slip under the US 44 bridge. Next is a water treatment plant on your left. But after that, the Nemasket reveals itself as a pretty little river that weaves and wanders. There are many homes above the left shore but most are screened by trees and bushes and do little to interfere with the scenery. The banks are far apart, indicating this was once a considerably larger river, but the channel is narrow as it curves through weeds and thick grasses. These plants provide nesting habitat for ducks and geese, and you are likely to see many birds throughout this trip. We've also seen numerous great blue herons here, along with hawks, ospreys, and the

Old mill stonework and a fish ladder highlight the Nemasket launch site.

usual songbirds of wetlands such as red-winged blackbirds, kingbirds, yellow warblers, swallows, and yellowthroats.

Even with little paddling, you will probably reach the first bridge in less than an hour. This is the low Plymouth Street bridge, built of rough fieldstone. The bridge is believed to date from about 1850 and at this writing is closed to traffic. Although a bit difficult for canoeists, it is an appealing look back into history. There are five narrow openings, with the center one usually offering the best passage. In higher water, canoeists may have to lie down to slip through. If unsure of passage, you can carry around on the right.

The river meanders even more beyond this bridge and the next one, which is at Murdock Street, the alternative take-out. You pass under the same power line several times, zigzagging through a swampy segment that can be maddening if you are in a hurry, but delightful if you enjoy seeing birds. When the channel runs near the wooded banks, note the many big beech trees. They are great specimens. Oaks and pines also tower over the water. Together these trees provide good backgrounds in spring and summer and wonderful colors in autumn.

There are few homes visible from the river beyond Murdock Street, just trees, bushes, swamp plants, and birds. We've also seen many turtles, including an immense snapping turtle, in this segment. After you pass under a railroad bridge, it is only another 15 minutes or so, but with several more bends and twists, until the Nemasket ends by flowing into the Taunton.

Just like that, you go from a narrow, weaving stream into a wide, flat river, a much straighter river. But you are still floating between stands of tall, impressive trees. The change can feel good as you float the remaining mile down to Titicut Street. If planning to take out at this bridge, you have a choice. The easier take-out is on the left, just before the bridge. However, you may want to add still another perspective to your trip and run the riffles under the bridge. They are stronger than anything you found on the Nemasket. If going through the riffles, after you pass beneath the bridge, swing out of the current and then take out, also on the left side of the river.

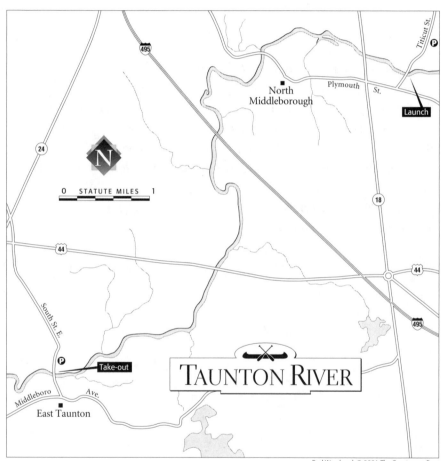

495

Titicut St.

P

North
Middleborough

Plymouth St.

Launch

24

N

STATUTE MILES

0   1

18

44

44

495

South St. E.

P

Take-out

TAUNTON RIVER

Middleboro Ave.

East Taunton

11

Taunton River

North Middleborough to East Taunton

Put-in Point	Take-out Point	Approximate Distance	Approximate Trip Time	Condition of Water	Portages
Titicut Street bridge	South Street bridge	7½ miles	2½–3 hours	Smooth, few riffles	None

If you like your canoeing on the leisurely side, with time to look around and plenty to look at, give the Taunton River in southeastern Massachusetts a try. The 7½-mile trip described here is one of the easiest in this book, and it offers a succession of natural attractions, particularly trees. On this stretch of the Taunton, from east of North Middleborough to East Taunton, you float through impressive old forests. These stands are intriguing both for their great variety of trees and for individual specimens, several of which are towering monarchs that must be upwards of 200 years old.

The Taunton, of course, is much older than any of its trees and has been canoed for many centuries. Now part of the Wampanoag Commemorative Canoe Passage, honoring Native Americans who long paddled this waterway, the river is still very appealing despite being in a heavily settled region. It is easy enough to be recommended for beginners and family groups. The current is moderate and steady, and there are no portages and no rapids, although occasional riffles beneath bridges will keep you alert. Even with brief stops to look over the trees and a lunch break, this stretch is easily canoed in 2½ to 3 hours.

For a longer trip, you can combine this paddle with the Nemasket

River (see Trip 10). By floating the Nemasket first and then doing the Taunton, you will go approximately 13¼ miles.

Access

Your take-out will be beside a power station in East Taunton. From US 44, turn south onto Orchard Street, just east of MA 24. Orchard Street soon merges with South Street. Follow South Street 1½ miles to the river and leave a car beside the power station on your left. Note a large brick building, now the River Bend Condominiums, on the opposite side of the river. That building and the bridge will be your landmarks for the take-out.

To haul your canoe to the put-in, return to US 44, then go east to MA 18–MA 28, turn left (north) and drive 2 miles to Plymouth Street, which you then take right (east) a short distance to Titicut Street. Follow Titicut Street left (north) until it reaches the river. The best put-in is on the near side of the river, to the right of the road. If you wish to avoid the riffles under the bridge, you can put in over a guardrail on the left. However, leaving a car at this end of the trip requires parking several hundred feet beyond the bridge, on the right.

The River

At the put-in, you may face an obstacle right away. A string of rocks directly under the Titicut Street bridge forms a riffle. In high water, you can run it in the center, but when the water is down you may have to pull over to the left and line your canoe a few yards while walking on rocks at the foot of the abutment. Launching from the west side of the bridge avoids this riffle, but running it can be fun, and lining is easy.

The river is broad, smooth, and lined on both sides by thick woods, a condition that continues throughout most of the trip. There are few houses or cottages on the banks. In fact, only a few buildings of any kind are visible until you near your take-out in East Taunton.

In summer, much of the distance between Titicut Street and the MA 18–MA 28 bridge is decorated with the showy purple spikes of

The Taunton River is wide and smooth, and easy for families.

pickerelweed, a plant that thrives at the shoreline. Look closely in the shallow water at the base of the flower stalks; you are likely to see numerous big bullfrogs drowsily soaking up the sunshine, usually with just their heads above water. Make this trip on a summer evening, and you won't have to look for the frogs. You'll hear their bellowing chant long before you reach them.

Wildlife can be abundant along the Taunton, even though the river runs through a heavily populated part of the state. On one midsummer cruise here, we saw a mink, a great horned owl, several red-tailed hawks, a pair of mallard ducks, a wide assortment of songbirds, a sparrow hawk, several noisy kingfishers, and a mother wood duck that stashed her two half-grown youngsters in the weeds and then flopped along in front of our canoe for a quarter of a mile trying to lead us astray. On a spring float, we saw many great blue herons, an osprey, and barn swallows that had nests under nearly every bridge. In addition, raccoon tracks often dot the banks, and the shells of freshwater mussels, the object of the coons' forays, can be easy to find. You can also see muskrat tunnels in the banks when the water level is down.

But you are far more certain of seeing the big trees. These are close enough to the water so that you can pull over for a close look at almost any time. Many maples reach out over the river, their brilliant foliage making the Taunton an excellent autumn trip. Half a dozen species of oaks are here, too, including several gigantic swamp white oaks. There are groves of beeches, birches, pines, and hemlocks, and a great many hickory and walnut trees. The free nuts are another bonus on fall trips. Fall is the time for seeing the relatively rare tupelo, or black gum tree, also, for then its leaves turn a fiery scarlet. The smooth floating gives you time to take a good look at all the trees.

Your first riffles after the Titicut Street bridge come about 2 miles from the start as you near a concrete bridge. These amount to very little, however; you can easily slip through the center. Just beyond the bridge, on the left, is a string of majestic old maples, each one a giant. You'll next come to a stretch of very shallow water punctuated with large boulders that are easy to maneuver past. Then you will pass beneath another bridge, float over more riffles, and in several more minutes reach the double bridges of I-495. This point is roughly 3½ miles from your start. The next several miles, during which you paddle under the US 44 bridge and on toward East Taunton, are pleasant and easy. The smooth water divides delightful forests with only an occasional patch of boulders to negotiate. There are a few open fields below the US 44 bridge, and some homes and farms are visible in the distance. You pass under only one more bridge in this segment.

Just before reaching your take-out at the South Street Bridge in East Taunton, you'll see a business complex on the left side. This is your signal to pull over to the right. The take-out, up a path on a rather steep bank, is not particularly easy and there are more ripples pulling you toward the bridge, so be sure to approach the bridge close to the right shore. After taking out, you may want to take a closer look at the towering brick structure, once a mill building, and the extensive stonework laid up on the banks in the days when the Taunton River was harnessed by industry. The stonework, like the venerable old trees, invites closer inspection.

PART II
Rhode Island

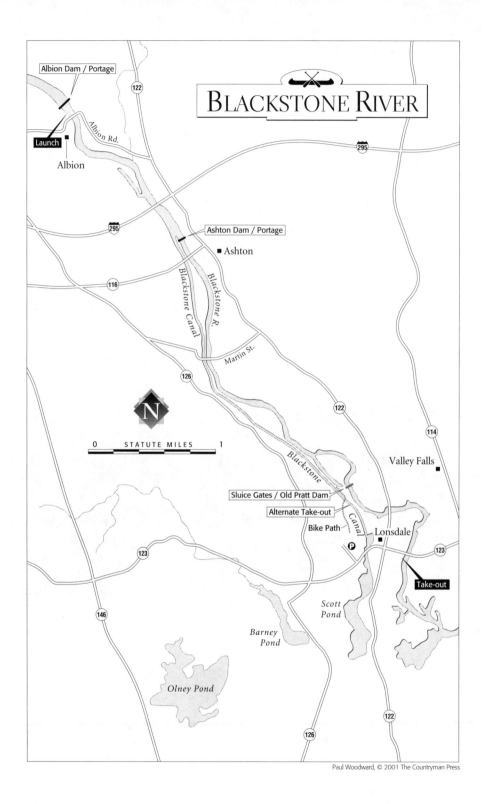

BLACKSTONE RIVER

Albion Dam / Portage

122

295

Launch ■
Albion

Albion Rd.

295

116

Ashton Dam / Portage
■ Ashton

Blackstone Canal

Blackstone R.

Martin St.

126

122

N

114

STATUTE MILES

0   1

Blackstone

Valley Falls ■

Sluice Gates / Old Pratt Dam

Alternate Take-out

Bike Path

Canal

Lonsdale ■

123

P

Take-out

123

Scott
Pond

146

Barney
Pond

Olney Pond

126

122

Paul Woodward, © 2001 The Countryman Press

12
Blackstone River

Albion to Lonsdale

Put-in Point	Take-out Point	Approximate Distance	Approximate Trip Time	Condition of Water	Portages
Albion Dam	John Street, Lonsdale	5 miles	2½ hours	Mostly smooth	Ashton Dam, Pratt Dam

Canoe trips on the Blackstone River in northern Rhode Island continue to get better and better. Once considered among America's most polluted rivers because of the mills and factories along its shores, the Blackstone now runs cleaner than at any time in a century. In recent years, trout have even been stocked in portions of the river, something that would have seemed absolutely ludicrous a few decades ago.

In addition, continued development of the Blackstone River State Park in this area, particularly where the river is joined by the historic Blackstone Canal, makes this a thoroughly pleasant canoeing experience. You can now get around one dam by going a short distance into the canal and using new stone steps, and if you wish, you can avoid another dam and a possible long carry by taking the canal a couple of miles. Still more improvements are coming: Scheduled for completion in the near future is a portage around the old Pratt Dam, which has stymied canoeists for years and dumped many who tried to paddle through the dam's treacherous sluice gates.

The Blackstone River begins in Massachusetts (see Trip 5), enters Rhode Island just north of Woonsocket, and runs through Pawtucket and eventually into Narragansett Bay. In the early days, the river was the primary means of both transportation and power for the area. Unfortunately, the many mills it spawned during the textile boom of years ago nearly destroyed the river, and it took great efforts on the part of hundreds of volunteers, along with the closing of most of the old mills, to bring the river back to life. Now, canoeing the broad river is enjoyable again. As the state park work progresses, more access points will be made and portages will become easier.

Until a planned put-in below Manville is built, I suggest starting at Albion and running to Lonsdale. That is a distance of about 5 miles. To see more of the river and its resurgent wildlife, you can extend the trip on both ends: by going upriver from Albion to the Manville Dam, then returning, and at the end of your trip by floating into the Lonsdale Marsh before returning to the take-out.

If you do not go upriver from Albion, the only portages are an easy one at Ashton and a longer one around Pratt Dam near Lonsdale. Pratt Dam does have open sluice gates that some canoeists run, but doing so can be dangerous and spills are frequent. This should not be attempted by inexperienced canoeists.

The Blackstone's current is usually fairly strong, but the only rocky water, other than at Pratt Dam, is just below the other dams and beneath the RI 116 and Martin Street bridges. These areas are usually mere riffles but occasionally increase up to Class II rapids.

In summer, when the current has slowed a bit, it's also possible to make a down-and-back paddle from Albion to the canal, do some exploring, and then return to your put-in. Such a trip requires only one vehicle and involves no portages, but it does miss some good sections of river. Still another alternative is to take out at the far end of the canal, using the parking lot for a bike path. Such a trip would eliminate the Pratt Dam problem but also miss the faster sections.

Access

Your take-out is in Lonsdale, below the bridge for RI 123 (John Street). Take a dirt lane, badly rutted at this writing, across from the entrance to the old Lonsdale Drive-in Theater. This lane, which is state-owned, is also due for improvement and will become an official boat ramp. It ends at the river and provides space for leaving a car.

Before going to your put-in, it may be a good idea to take a look at the Pratt Dam so you can better decide whether to try running it, carrying around, or bypassing it on the canal. From the take-out, go west on RI 123 a short distance beyond RI 122 to the Blackstone River State Park entrance, on your right. Walk a paved bike path to its first river view; from here you can see how much water is churning through the old dam's open gates.

To reach the put-in, return on RI 123 to RI 122, which you then follow north about $4\frac{1}{2}$ miles to Albion Road on the left. Follow Albion Road until it crosses the river. Just beyond the bridge is a gravel lane running to the right, toward the Albion Dam. The easiest spot to put in is just below the dam. However, in low water, this area might be too rocky and you may have to choose a place nearer the Albion Road bridge.

If planning to add a paddle upriver toward Manville, put in just above the dam.

The River

Before starting downriver, you might want to go upriver for a while. The $1\frac{1}{2}$-mile stretch between Albion and Manville is flatwater with wooded shores. We canoe it sometimes just for the wildlife—herons and sandpipers stalk the shallows, kingfishers rattle across the river, and orioles and thrushes sing from the shoreline trees. There also are big snapping turtles in this section, along with a great many bullfrogs.

Below Albion Dam, you quickly pass under Albion Road and then under a railroad bridge. This section is the best trout-fishing segment; signs along the shore state the regulations. A huge brick building on the right, originally a mill and now the Highland Falls Condominiums complex, is about all you can see of the village of Albion from the water.

For most of the run to the next dam, you paddle between attractive shores accented with large trees, vibrant mountain laurel thickets, and rock outcroppings. The water is generally smooth and easy.

After passing under the high double bridge for I-295, you are nearing the Ashton Dam. Look for stonework and guardrails on the right—they mark the entrance to the Blackstone Canal. The canal begins just before the dam, within sight of the towering, arching viaduct for RI 116.

Since the development of the Blackstone River State Park, it's an easy matter to enter the canal. But you will be in the canal for only a few moments if you intend to return to the river and paddle down to Pratt Dam. Once in the canal, look on the left, at the end of a stone retaining wall, for steps that enable canoeists to carry their boats back to the river.

It is important at this point to decide whether you want to try running the sluice gates at Pratt Dam, 2 miles ahead, or tackle the still-difficult portage at the dam. If you'd rather play it safe, stay in the canal, which was built in the 1820s and still shows much of the original stonework. In all but extremely high or low water the canal provides an easy paddle all the way to Lonsdale. In high water, you may have to portage around the Martin Street bridge. The canal eventually runs beneath buildings in Lonsdale. Follow it until passing under a low green bridge built for the bike path. Then take out on the left, carry down a path that runs beside the canal, and return to the river. It's not a particularly easy portage—you have to carry down a steep enbankment—but it might be preferable to running Pratt Dam, which you can see as soon as you climb the canal bank.

For those who choose the river route from the Ashton Dam, you'll have a longer route because the river makes two sweeping curves to the left. There are "boney" areas beneath both the RI 116 and Martin Street bridges, and you'll have to pick your way through a couple of other "rock gardens." For the most part, though, it's a fairly easy paddle until reaching Pratt Dam.

You reach the dam just as the river makes a sharp turn left. There are several sluice gates, and the river roars through them with whitewater fury. All canoeists planning to run the dam should pull out on the right and walk ahead to check the openings very carefully for branches or other debris that might be caught in the passages. More than one canoeist has been dumped by such obstacles, and a dumping here, with the water crashing through the narrow gates, can be very dangerous. Unfortunately, at present, carrying around the dam is difficult because of the high retaining walls on both sides of the river. Park

A canoe portage is planned around the old Pratt Dam.

plans include building a portage around the left side of the dam, incorporating the carry into an extension of the bike path that is expected to cross the river on the old dam. The new portage will surely be welcomed by all who have had to deal with this dam in the past.

When the sluice gates are clear, the run through can be exhilarating, even though you are likely to get doused by the backwash and standing waves just below the dam. Remember, this should not be attempted by canoeists paddling alone or those without whitewater expertise.

Just beyond the dam you will pass under the RI 122 bridge and begin making the horseshoe curve around what was the Lonsdale Drive-in Theater.

The next bridge is for RI 123 (John Street) and just beyond is your take-out point on the right, but you may want to continue into Lonsdale Marsh, about half a mile ahead. The marsh is one of the "wildest" wetlands in this part of the state. The many coves are home to ducks, geese, swans, egrets, herons, rails, bitterns, marsh wrens, red-winged blackbirds, and assorted other birds. With the smooth water, a return to your take-out is easy.

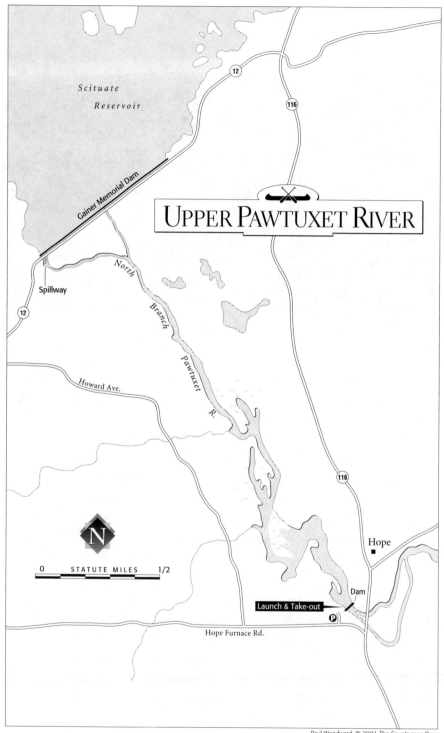

Scituate
Reservoir

Gainer Memorial Dam

12

116

UPPER PAWTUXET RIVER

Spillway

North Branch Pawtuxet R.

12

Howard Ave.

116

N

0   STATUTE MILES   1/2

Hope

Dam

Launch & Take-out

Ⓟ

Hope Furnace Rd.

Paul Woodward, © 2001 The Countryman Press

13

Upper Pawtuxet River

Scituate

Put-in and Take-out Point	Approximate Distance	Approximate Trip Time	Condition of Water	Portages
Hope Furnace Road, Hope	4½ miles	3–3½ hours	Mostly smooth	None

For a short trip requiring only one vehicle and a few hours, the upper part of the Pawtuxet River's North Branch is hard to beat. This 4½-mile round trip from the village of Hope, on the Scituate-Coventry line, to the high dam of the Scituate Reservoir can be done in 3 hours or so, depending, of course, on the water level and current. It's a clean, pretty river with plenty of birds, and the current is usually smooth enough that paddling upstream is not difficult. In early spring, however, or in seasons of heavy rain, when the huge reservoir is filled, the current can be quite fast, particularly in the upper stretch nearest the dam.

This section of the Pawtuxet is often called the Hope River. It flows directly from the reservoir, and that keeps the water clean and cold enough that trout thrive here. There are some homes along the river, particularly at the lower end, but also plenty of woods and wildlife. The best time for canoeing this river might be June, after the torrents of spring have subsided, before the low-water doldrums of midsummer arrive, and while the thickets of mountain laurel along the shores are in bloom. If possible, go during the week, when river traffic is light.

Before launching it might be a good idea to take a look at the spillway at the southwestern end of the reservoir dam, named Gainer Dam, on RI 12. If water is pouring over the spillway, you can expect the river current to be fairly swift and strong. If the spillway is dry you'll have smooth water and possibly a few areas of low water.

Access

After checking the spillway, take RI 12 east a short distance to RI 116, turn right (south) and drive the few miles to Hope, cross the river and take the first right after the bridge, Hope Furnace Road. Almost immediately you reach the Pawtuxet River Fishing Access, where you can leave your car and launch just above an old dam.

The River

The first section above the launch site is wide and pondlike, with shallow coves that frequently hold ducks, geese, and herons. You'll see homes on the left shore and a beach area on the right. The river quickly makes a bend to the left, then two abrupt rights. In some of the broad areas it can be tricky to stay in the main channel; watch the current closely.

Kingfishers, swallows, swifts, red-winged blackbirds, and other birds can usually be found in these pond areas. Soon, however, the waterway narrows (near the only homes on the right shore) and becomes more streamlike. Muskrats and squirrels may be found here, and once a deer plunged through the river ahead of my canoe. There have recently been some signs of beavers' presence as well.

After making a sharp left bend at a private beach with a sign identifying it as Frosty Valley, you'll pass a cluster of homes on the left, then move into what is probably the prettiest section of the river. Trees crowd both shores, laurel blossoms gleam white and pink (in June), and boulders dot the river and shoreline. Although some of the boulders are large, the water remains smooth and there is ample room to maneuver past the rocks.

You'll pass one more complex of homes and cabins on the left, then paddle through a shallow stretch that might be scratchy in extremely low water, and fast in high water. It's a short segment, though, and soon you will be back in easy paddling. Next you reach a fork; the main

Tranquil forest shades much of the Upper Pawtuxet.

channel goes straight ahead, but take a look at the left branch. In high water it leads to rapids and an impressive falls; in low water it is all deadwater and leads only to dry rocks. This is the channel that carries excess water flowing over the dam spillway.

The main river channel runs directly to the high dam; you can see the gatehouse high above you and a stairway running down the earthen dam to a roadway below. You may not be able to paddle all the way to the dam if the current is strong, but you can see the dam as soon as you pass the confluence with the spillway channel.

Returning to your car is a simple matter of turning around and floating back down the river.

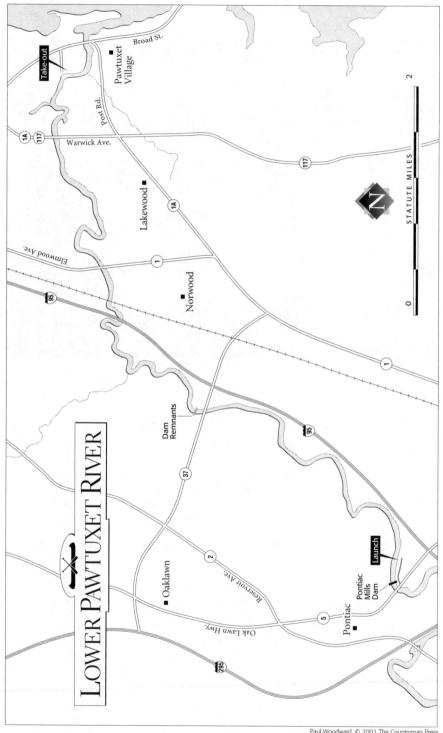

LOWER PAWTUXET RIVER

Take-out

Broad St.

Pawtuxet
Village

Post Rd.

1A
117

Warwick Ave.

Lakewood

1A

Elmwood Ave.

1

95

Norwood

N

STATUTE MILES

0   2

Dam
Remnants

1

95

37

Oaklawn

2

Reservoir Ave.

Launch

Pontiac
Mills
Dam

Oak Lawn Hwy.

5

Pontiac

295

2

14

Lower Pawtuxet River

Warwick to Cranston

Put-in Point	Take-out Point	Approximate Distance	Approximate Trip Time	Condition of Water	Portages
Pontiac Mills	Pawtuxet Village	8 miles	2½–3 hours	Mostly smooth	None

The Pawtuxet River in central Rhode Island is yet another waterway that was once abused terribly, when it ran dozens of mills, but has regained much of its charm through cleanup efforts and changes in its uses. It now provides some of the best nearby canoeing for people in the heavily populated Providence-Cranston-Warwick area, offering several miles of portage-free paddling.

This is the lower Pawtuxet—you'll take out in Pawtuxet Village, near where the river empties into the upper reaches of Narragansett Bay—and it is quite removed from the idyllic surroundings of the upper Pawtuxet (Trip 13) in rural Scituate. For most of this trip, you are floating between two cities, as the river provides the boundary between Warwick on your right and Cranston on your left. Still, you can get the feeling that you are much farther from the industrialized metropolitan sections than you actually are because tall trees flank the river nearly all the way. The largest drawback is not in what you see but in what you hear: Highways are so close that traffic noise is unavoidable. Still, the paddling is easy, the current steady, and the trip very pleasant. This is a river to choose when looking for a few hours of leisurely floating.

The river is wide and though relatively shallow, it holds its water quite well and can usually be canoed throughout the summer. Spring, however, is probably the best time, because of the birds. On a May trip here we found scarlet tanagers, orioles, warblers, and other songbirds in the trees, and swallows and chimney swifts swooped over the water. There were numerous ducks and geese along the river as well, and sometimes herons and egrets stalked the sandbars, looking for frogs and tiny fish.

Although in most river conditions there are no portages to be concerned with, canoeists should be aware that when the water level is low, two spots in close succession just beyond the RI 37 bridges midway in the trip might require some extra care. They are the remains of old dams and can usually be floated over; but if the water is low, they might have to be carried over or around. Neither portage is difficult.

Access

The put-in is just below the old Pontiac Mills dam off RI 5 near Warwick Mall. Turn off the highway at the Greenwich Village Apartments. Drive to the far left end of the parking lot. The put-in is across a grassy field to the left, where a path leads to the river.

To leave a vehicle at the take-out at Rhodes-on-the-Pawtuxet, a local landmark that has served as a gathering place for dances, weddings, and other functions for generations, go south on RI 5, cross I-95, and then take the first right for access onto I-95 North. Follow I-95 to RI 37, take RI 37 east to Route 1 (Post Road) north. Follow Post Road as RI 1 changes to RI 1A into Pawtuxet Village, turn left onto Broad Street, cross the river, and then take Rhodes Place left to the parking lot near a large white building on the riverbank. This is Rhodes-on-the-Pawtuxet, a can't-miss take-out as you float down the river.

The River

Back at the put-in, take a moment to look upstream after launching. You are just below the dam for Pontiac Mills. Back in the 1800s the Pawtuxet powered many such mills with these dams. Discharges from the mills and from other sources once polluted the river so badly it was

The Pawtuxet River now draws many canoeists and kayakers.

virtually an open sewer, but that is no longer the case. The water is not yet clear, and on your trip you will pass discoloration from the Cranston water treatment plant, but the river is considerably cleaner than in the past and continues to improve each year. Your trip down the river also improves as you proceed.

Soon after you begin, you find yourself floating just below busy I-95 (in a couple of places the river was straightened a bit to accommodate the highway's construction). For the most part, you hear rather than see the traffic above. After looping away from the highway briefly, you return. Here, you might see through trees on the left the guard towers for the Adult Corrections Institutions, the state prison. In summer, when leaves are fully developed, you can easily float past the prison without knowing it is there.

The first bridges you reach, less than an hour from the put-in, are the double spans of RI 37. Just beyond are the low obstacles remaining from removed dams. As mentioned earlier, they can usually be floated over. If uneasy about attempting this, carry around on the right. This is rarely necessary.

You now return to I-95, but of more concern is the discharge coming in from the left from the Cranston water treatment plant. This is the least attractive segment of the entire trip; fortunately, the discoloration is quickly diffused. And so is the odor. There are glimpses of some businesses on the right shore, but for the most part you are still paddling between columns of tall trees, including impressive sycamores, relatively rare in Rhode Island.

The river curves considerably before you pass under the I-95 bridge. Now you are entering the best segment. You'll quickly float under a railroad bridge and the RI 28 bridge, then most of the noise dies away and you can more fully appreciate the setting. You may see people walking along the right shore in part of Belmont Park, one of several areas along the river beautified in recent years for the public. The river is smooth and pretty here; you'll probably want to drift instead of paddling.

After passing under a footbridge and gated road bridge, both part of an old industrial complex, you are nearing the RI 117 bridge, your last bridge. From here, it is an easy float down to the huge white structure that is Rhodes-on-the-Pawtuxet. The take-out is at a concrete slab just as you reach the building.

15

Pettaquamscutt (Narrow) River

Narragansett

Put-in Point	Take-out Points	Approximate Distance	Approximate Trip Time	Condition of Water	Portages
Gilbert Stuart Landing	Narrow River Landing	4½ miles	2 hours	Smooth (tidal)	None
Gilbert Stuart Landing	Cement Bridge	5¾ miles	2½ hours	Smooth (tidal)	None

In canoeing the Pettaquamscutt, or Narrow River, as it is known to most Rhode Islanders, you will travel through a 200-year span in less than 3 hours. Your start will be beside an 18th-century landmark that features clapboard-covered buildings and a grinding waterwheel, and you can end the trip riding the ocean surf in the company of sleek, modern powerboats.

The Pettaquamscutt, only about 6 miles long, runs parallel to Narragansett Bay entirely within the town of Narragansett. This area is just above southeastern Rhode Island's most popular beaches and the fishing villages of Point Judith and Galilee. The Pettaquamscutt is a tidal river, so you should check a tide chart before attempting this trip. Canoeing 6 miles against the tide can be hard work, but floating with it makes this trip one of the easier ones in Rhode Island. To catch the outgoing current, start shortly after high tide, which is about 5 minutes earlier in Narragansett than at Newport. Tidal data for Newport is given in local newspapers.

Access

You have a choice of take-outs. You can drive US 1 to Middle Bridge Road, turn east and drive for about 1½ miles, turn left onto Pollock

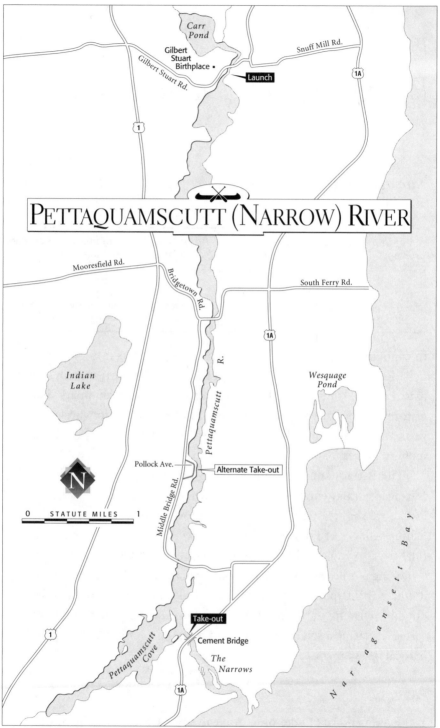

Pettaquamscutt (Narrow) River

Carr Pond

Gilbert Stuart Birthplace ▪

Gilbert Stuart Rd.

Snuff Mill Rd.

Launch

1A

1

Mooresfield Rd.

Bridgetown Rd.

South Ferry Rd.

1A

Indian Lake

Pettaquamscutt R.

Wesquage Pond

N

Pollock Ave.

Alternate Take-out

Middle Bridge Rd.

0 STATUTE MILES 1

Narragansett Bay

1

Take-out

Pettaquamscutt Cove

Cement Bridge

The Narrows

1A

Paul Woodward, © 2001 The Countryman Press

Avenue, and park at the Narrow River Fishing Area, a state-owned landing. Or you can continue driving across Middle Bridge, turn right onto US 1A, and leave a car beside the next bridge, which is officially named Governor Sprague Bridge but is usually referred to locally as Cement Bridge. River access from the highway is good just before the bridge on the right, and just after the bridge, on the left. There is more parking on the left side of the highway but take-out is easier on the right. The extra stretch of river between the Narrow River landing and Cement Bridge adds only about 1¼ miles of canoeing and makes it much easier to explore a large cove between the two sites. Also, Cement Bridge serves as a more convenient take-out if you wish to paddle on out to the ocean, which is less than a mile away.

To reach the put-in, return to US 1 and drive north to Gilbert Stuart Road (just south of RI 138) and turn east. Immediately after Gilbert Stuart Road crosses a small stream at the bottom of a steep hill, look on the right for a sign indicating Gilbert Stuart Landing. This landing will be your parking lot and launch site. Stuart names dominate the area because Gilbert Stuart, one of America's foremost portrait painters of the post-Revolution era, was born in the farmhouse just across the road from the landing. It is worth taking time to visit the restored home and mills of Stuart's youth either before or after your canoe trip. A guided tour of the buildings and grounds is available for a small fee. In addition to the house, with its 18h-century furnishings and numerous reproductions of Stuart's most famous paintings, you will also get a look at a gristmill, an Indian burial ground, and a waterwheel that still turns, keeping the snuff mill on the ground floor of the house operable. This snuff mill, the first in New England, was constructed by Stuart's father shortly after he arrived in 1751. Gilbert Stuart was born in 1755 and lived here until he was 13 years old.

The River

At your start, the Pettaquamscutt (an Indian word meaning "big, round rock" and referring to a huge granite ledge just west of here, but not visible from the water) is not only narrow but also very shallow. Gilbert

Stuart Brook joins another stream here in forming the river. You may have to line your canoe a short distance before hopping in. Quickly, though, you will emerge onto a large pond and you'll be on your way. The water is generally clear here and the paddling is easy. At this point, you will not be affected much by the tides.

Paddle toward the narrow gap on the south side of the pond. Once through this gap, which is shallow but canoeable even at low tide, you will begin to feel the effects of the tide. You will be in another pondlike expanse that may make you wonder why anybody would nickname the Pettaquamscutt the Narrow River. This section is perhaps the prettiest of the trip, with wooded shores on both sides. There are several houses along the left bank, but the right side resembles a park, with stately trees parading down a long slope to the water. If you are floating the out-going tide and are not confronted with the strong headwinds that sometimes sweep upriver, you will reach a bridge in slightly more than an hour from your start. This is the Bridgetown Road bridge.

Beyond this first bridge, the river narrows considerably and is flanked on both sides by houses, many of which feature docks and a boat or two. On summer weekends you may find the boating traffic in this area too heavy for pleasant canoeing. You will continue to see houses along the right shore for the remaining miles to Narrow River landing. The left shore, however, soon opens into an area dotted with tiny estuaries. Many of these can be explored by canoe at high tide. When the tide is out, the exposed mudflats attract numerous egrets, herons, sandpipers, and other shorebirds. When the next bridge, Middle Bridge, comes into view, begin looking on the right shore for the boat ramp, if this is to be your take-out point.

If the water is low as you near Middle Bridge, keep to the left to re-main in the main channel. The right side is quite shallow. Note, too, that you may have to dodge fishing lines as you pass under the bridge. This is one of the area's most popular fishing spots, particularly in early spring when the flatfish are hitting. Indeed, it is rare to see this bridge without at least one angler. Flounder and striped bass also are caught in the river, and its upper reaches near Gilbert Stuart's birthplace are famous locally for the annual run of buckies, or river herring.

Take time to paddle around Pettaquamscutt Cove on the Narrow River.

Beyond Middle Bridge, where water traffic usually picks up because of a kayak rental, the river's main channel curves left, toward Cement Bridge. First, though, you may want to spend some time exploring Pettaquamscutt Cove and its islands off to the right. The cove is shallow and bird life around the low islands is usually abundant, so a leisurely side trip can be most enjoyable. In 1999 a pair of ospreys had a nest on an old duck hunter's blind, an unusually low place for an osprey nest.

Once you reach Cement Bridge, you have another option. You can take out immediately just before the bridge, on the left, or proceed under the bridge and take out on the right, depending on where you parked. Or you can follow the river all the way to the sea and then return. There are some rocks at the mouth, called The Narrows, and generally plenty of surf. Experienced canoeists often come here in summer for canoe-surfing, paddling out through the waves and riding them back in. In rough seas, though, this is a sport best left to the experts.

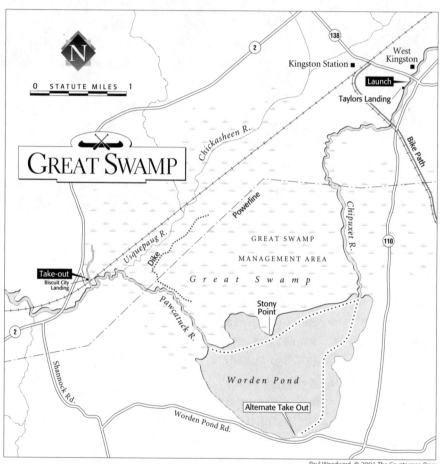

N

0 STATUTE MILES 1

GREAT SWAMP

2

138

Kingston Station ■

West
Kingston
■

Launch

Taylors Landing

Bike Path

Chickasheen R.

Powerline

GREAT SWAMP

MANAGEMENT AREA

Chipuxet R.

110

Usquepaug R.

Dike

Great Swamp

Take-out
Biscuit City
Landing

Pawcatuck R.

Stony
Point

2

Shannock Rd.

Worden Pond

Alternate Take Out

Worden Pond Rd.

Paul Woodward, © 2001 The Countryman Press

16

Great Swamp

South Kingstown

Put-in Point	Take-out Points	Approximate Distance	Approximate Trip Time	Condition of Water	Portages
Taylor's Landing	Worden Pond Road	5 1/2 miles	2–2 1/2 hours	Smooth, open pond	None
Taylor's Landing	Biscuit City Road	7 miles	4–4 1/2 hours	Smooth, open pond	None

The Great Swamp, located in the southern part of Rhode Island, provides perhaps the most intriguing canoe trip in the state. The trip is an excursion into hidden junglelike retreats that cannot be reached any other way. Here you will float into a vast state-owned management area on one river, paddle across a shallow but wide pond, and then finish your trip on another river that snakes its way through dense vine-draped vegetation. There will be no doubt in your mind why this area is called Great Swamp.

Two routes are available. The full 7-mile trip includes portions of the Chipuxet and Charles Rivers and Worden Pond. A shorter version of about 5 1/2 miles takes the Chipuxet to Worden Pond, and then follows the pond's southern shoreline to a landing. The shorter trip takes only about 2 1/2 hours, but it misses the fascinating atmosphere of the winding Charles, as well as a lunch break on a picturesque point jutting out into the pond and a stopover at a wildlife marsh where ospreys, impressive fish-eating hawks, can be spotted.

Access

The put-in for both trips is Taylor's Landing, a state launching area on RI 138 in West Kingston. If you are making the short trip, you reach the take-out by driving east on RI 138 from Taylor's Landing a few yards to RI 110, and then going south to Worden Pond Road, which you follow west to the landing at the pond's edge.

If you are making the full 7-mile trip, drive west from Taylor's Landing to RI 2, turn south, and continue around the swamp to Biscuit City Road. A short drive on this secondary road will take you to a state landing beside a railroad track. There is plenty of room here for your car.

The River

Back at Taylor's Landing, you launch on the Chipuxet, a stream that is very narrow for the first several hundred yards. There are similar areas ahead, too, so it is best to make this trip in spring before the heavy summer growth reduces the river's width. Water depth remains fairly constant throughout the warmer months, however, so you can canoe here during the summer if you don't mind pushing your way through bushes occasionally. Less than ½ mile from its brushy beginning, the Chipuxet opens into a pleasant little river. The current will carry your canoe along, and all you have to do is steer around the numerous turns. There are no rapids here or anywhere else on this trip, no carries, and very few rocks to worry about. You occasionally come to logs and blow-downs, but they present few problems. Egrets, herons, ducks, geese, and songbirds frequent the river. In spring, the more open, marshy areas are virtual waterfowl nurseries, and you are likely to see many families of ducks and geese here. You are also likely to see signs of beavers, such as gnawed trees along the shore; ahead you will find a lodge and dam.

A new bridge built for a bicycle path along an old railroad bed is your first landmark. After making several sweeping turns you reach the next one, posts remaining from an old wooden boardwalk that used to follow a power line through the swamp. Here, in some places, taller trees edge the banks, but they soon give way again to smaller bushes.

In some places, the Great Swamp waterway is barely wide enough for a canoe.

Off to the sides are many shallow-water pockets that are ideal for the wood ducks and mallards you are likely to flush in spring. Muskrats and raccoons also abound in this area, and if you are quiet you might spot a deer coming down to the river for a drink. At this writing, a large beaver lodge stands along the right shore, but it can be concealed by the bushes. However, you can't miss the beavers' dam, just beyond the lodge. Unless the water level is low, though, you should be able to float over it.

When you reach Worden Pond, slightly more than 3 miles from your put-in, you are in for a different type of canoeing. This 1,000-acre pond is very shallow, but paddling across it can be work, particularly if you are heading into the wind, which seems to be the case more often than not. If your take-out is Worden Pond Road, follow the left shore around to the landing. If you are going on to Biscuit City Road, however, your immediate goal is Stony Point, a rock-ribbed finger of land slightly to the right of center as you face the pond. Stony Point points almost directly out toward the lone island in the pond. The point can be reached in a few minutes on a calm day, but on a windy day the journey may require a half hour or more of hard paddling.

Stony Point is a good place to stop even if you don't need a rest. The large round boulders scattered about make natural picnic tables, and laurel growing along the shore offers flowers in June and greenery all year. From the point, you will also have a panoramic view of the pond and the privately owned island, which features a small red cabin.

To resume your trip, paddle to the right, rounding the point, and head for another, less conspicuous point across a cove to the right. On the shore of the cove is a metal seaplane hangar left over from World War II; look for this building to get your bearing. After rounding the point beyond the hangar, follow the shore until reaching the mouth of the stream that you will take to exit the pond. On some maps it is called the Pawcatuck River, but most local residents call this section the Charles River and save the Pawcatuck name for a larger river (see Trip 19) farther west that is formed by the confluence of this stream and a couple of others.

By whatever name, this stream is a good practice course for back-watering and maneuvering around bends. It is nothing but turns, a succession of hairpins that can be a delight for the experienced canoeist but a challenge (or a headache) for the novice. The Charles is even narrower than the Chipuxet, and grapevines swing so low across the water you may have to duck occasionally to get through. Add the greenbrier vines that swarm over the shoreline bushes and you have a setting likely to conjure up images of monkeys, crocodiles, and other tropical animals. But relax; the only "wild animals" that may be a problem are mosquitoes. Fortunately, hundreds of swallows and other birds do their best to take care of that situation.

When the river swings near a high earthen dike and a cement platform on the right, tie up and climb the bank. This dike surrounds an expansive marsh created by the state as a wildlife refuge. The marsh is the home of numerous waterfowl as well as ospreys, which balance their bulky nests on power-line poles above the water. You can walk either direction on the dike for some distance if you wish. It is part of a well-known hiking trail. However, do not put your canoe in the marsh; it is for the birds only.

As you resume your trip on the Charles, you will find the river becoming even more crooked and you could run into problems with blowdowns or poison ivy, or both. It does become slightly wider than the stretch near the pond, though, making the maneuvering a bit easier. After passing more remains of the power-line boardwalk, you will paddle for some distance before meeting, on the right, another river that also has two names here: the Usquepaug and the Queens. Go left, with the current.

You will find the river wider the rest of the way, but there are still few straight stretches. When you see a railroad track on the right, you are nearing the take-out. In summer, foliage may obscure the railroad, but you'll be able to see the high wires that run above it. Don't swing into the first channel to the right; it's a dead end. Paddle to the left instead. After a few more turns, you will return to the railroad line a second time and soon after will see a very narrow brook entering, parallel to the railroad, on the right. Leave the main channel for this brook and follow it as it swings to the right and runs under the railroad tracks. Biscuit City Landing is on your left, just beyond the railroad tracks.

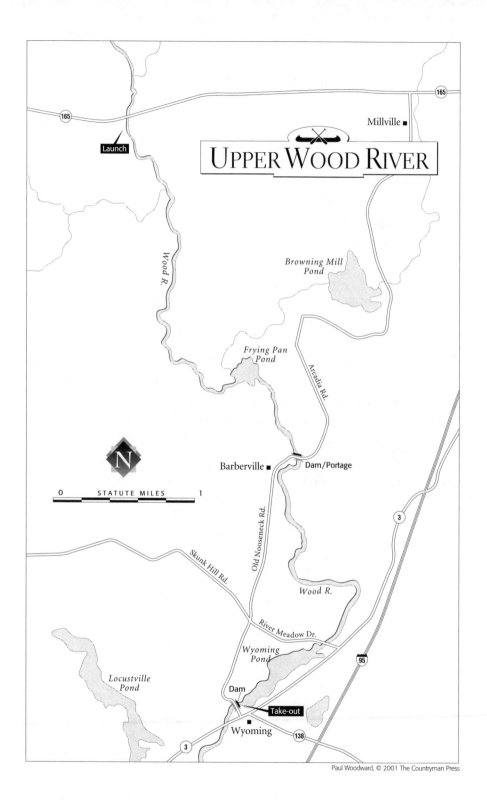

UPPER WOOD RIVER

Millville ■

Launch

165

165

Wood R.

Browning Mill
Pond

Frying Pan
Pond

Arcadia Rd.

N

0   STATUTE MILES   1

Barberville ■   Dam/Portage

Old Nooseneck Rd.

3

Skunk Hill Rd.

Wood R.

River Meadow Dr.

Wyoming
Pond

95

Locustville
Pond

Dam

Take-out

Wyoming ■

3   138

Paul Woodward, © 2001 The Countryman Press

17

Upper Wood River

Exeter to Wyoming

Put-in Point	Take-out Point	Approximate Distance	Approximate Trip Time	Condition of Water	Portages
RI 165 bridge	Wyoming Dam	5½ miles	3½–4 hours	Mostly smooth, some riffles	Barberville Dam

Ask any Rhode Island outdoor enthusiast for a good place to canoe in this state, and invariably the reply will begin, "Well, there's the Wood River . . ." The Wood deserves such recognition, for it has just about everything family canoeists look for. There is some fairly quick water and much smooth water, some open-pond paddling and some maneuvering around blowdowns, some shady forest stretches and some lush swamps.

Unfortunately, there also are several dams on the Wood River that interrupt the flow. Because of the dams and the problems they present, the Wood River is divided into two trips in this book, the upper Wood and the lower Wood (Trip 18), eliminating a central segment that includes too many dams and too many portages. These two trips present the river at its best, with only one portage on the upper Wood and one dam on the lower Wood that must be carried around.

The Wood River runs through the southwestern part of Rhode Island and eventually joins other streams in forming the Pawcatuck (see Trip 19) and flowing to the sea. Canoeing can begin as far north as the RI 165 bridge in Exeter and continue to Alton, which is just above the junction that forms the Pawcatuck. This upper Wood trip, however, terminates at Wyoming, where there is a convenient landing and parking area. It is approximately 5½ miles long and beautiful.

Access

To leave a car at the take-out, drive I-95 to Exit 3 and then follow RI 138 west into Wyoming. Just past the junction with RI 3, look for the Wyoming Fishing Area and landing at a dam on the right.

To reach the put-in, follow RI 3 about 5 miles north to RI 165, turn left, and drive RI 165 west about 4 miles to the river. Cross the bridge and immediately take a gravel lane to the left to a hunter checking station and parking area. You can launch behind the checking station.

The River

Even in spring the first stretch below RI 165 may involve some riffles and perhaps some scratchy going, as the river is narrow, rocky, and shallow. But soon you will find yourself on a quick little stream that winds through attractive woodlands. This is the state's best-known trout stream and you will undoubtedly meet fishermen here in April and May. Twice in the early going you will pass fishing access points on the right.

The area is good bird habitat, too, and you are likely to see many migrating warblers and ducks, and perhaps hear grouse drumming in the woods. Among the mammals that use the river are otters, deer, muskrats, raccoons, and beavers. Look for their tracks in the shoreline mud and sandbars. Beaver signs include gnawed bark on tree trunks and cone-shaped stumps. You may also run across a beaver dam or two; beavers frequently attempt to dam this river, but most of the dams eventually get taken out by spring freshets.

When you see the first house, a cabin in pines on the right, you are nearing a marshy area called Frying Pan Pond. This is a great place for waterfowl, herons, swallows, bullfrogs, and aquatic flowers. Just beyond, you'll begin seeing houses on both shores. The water here is wide and slow, indicating that you are approaching Barberville Dam. When you see a bridge, paddle to the left, the official take-out site. You will then have to carry across the bridge for relaunching into the river below a set of rapids. Do NOT try returning to the river immediately below the dam;

paddlers have been caught in the backwash and died attempting this. Members of the Wood-Pawcatuck Watershed Association (WPWA), an organization that works to protect all the waterways in this part of the state, can take out on the right, at a handicapped-accessible fishing pier just above the dam. Their portage is much shorter and easier. If you are not a member, you may want to stop at the building at the water's edge, the WPWA office, and pay the membership fee; it goes to a good cause and makes portages so much easier.

Regardless of which take-out you use, to relaunch, go to the SECOND parking spot beyond the bridge and follow a path down to the river. You will return to the water beyond the rapids, just below a point where an old sluiceway from the dam rejoins the main channel. The water here is usually fast but not dangerous and soon flattens out, although there is another brief riffles area as soon as you swing around a bend and pass below a house on the right.

This section of the river is as pretty as the first but not quite as wild. There are more homes here, particularly on the left, and you are likely to see more boats as well. It's an easy paddle or float to the next bridge, a low concrete structure, and as soon as you pass under this bridge you enter Wyoming Pond. The most direct route across the long but relatively narrow pond to your take-out, and the best way to avoid a strong headwind, is to follow the left shore.

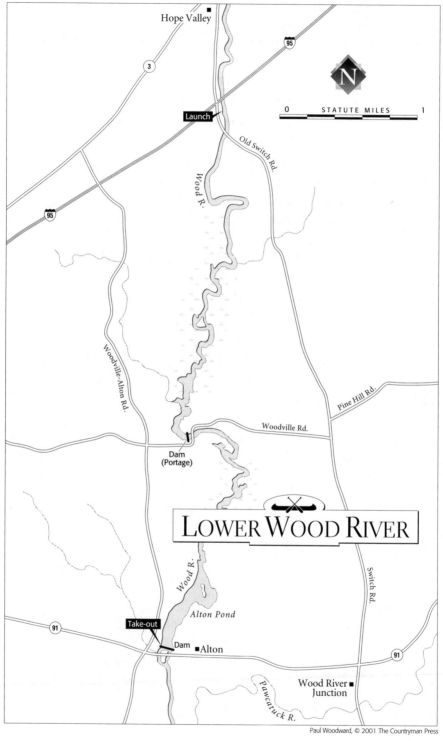

Hope Valley

95

3

Launch

Old Switch Rd.

Wood R.

95

Woodville-Alton Rd.

Pine Hill Rd.

Woodville Rd.

Dam
(Portage)

LOWER WOOD RIVER

Wood R.

Switch Rd.

Alton Pond

Take-out

91

Dam   ■ Alton

91

Pawcatuck R.

Wood River ■
Junction

18
Lower Wood River

Hope Valley to Alton

Put-in Point	Take-out Point	Approximate Distance	Approximate Trip Time	Condition of Water	Portages
Switch Road, Hope Valley	Alton Dam	6 miles	3½–4 hours	Mostly smooth	Woodville dam

The 6 miles from Hope Valley to Alton is considered by many to be the prettiest stretch of the Wood River, and possibly the most delightful canoeing area in Rhode Island. The water is clear and the current moderate; the shores wooded and wild. You will run into deadwater above a dam at Woodville and again in the pond above Alton, but the rest of the way it's simply a matter of floating around the bends and enjoying the scenery.

As with most rivers, the Wood does change complexion with the seasons. Spring trips here are the easiest, for the water is high and there will be few obstacles in your path except for the inevitable winter blowdowns, most of which are cut back rather quickly by canoe clubs and other environmental groups. In summer droughts, on the other hand, you may have to lift over some logs that you could float over in April. Perhaps the best times of all are May, when the river is alive with bird life, and June, when the shorelines are decorated with mountain laurel in spectacular bloom.

There is only one portage on this segment, a dam at Woodville, that is relatively long but not particularly difficult. It requires taking out on one side of the river, carrying across the bridge, and putting in on the other shore.

Access

Your take-out will be at state-owned Nathaniel Lewis Memorial Boat Landing on RI 91, just west of a dam in the village of Alton. After leaving a car here, you can reach your put-in point by following RI 91 east 1¾ miles, then going north (left) on Switch Road (called Hope Valley Road on some maps) about 4 miles until crossing the river. A landing will be a short distance ahead on the right.

The River

The early going is narrow and shallow, and you may have to maneuver past blowdowns. Quickly you reach the Switch Road bridge you just drove across; look up for the barn swallow nests usually plastered to the cement. If you are paddling here in spring and early summer, the swallows are likely to be swirling around you in their pursuit of insects.

Right away you will see mountain laurel along the shores, but the best laurel thickets are far ahead, beyond the Woodville dam. Blueberry bushes also grow on the banks, making delicious snacks available if you are passing through in July. Taller trees make up most of the shoreline, and you see only a handful of cottages, all on the left, until you reach Woodville.

In this first segment the river winds considerably, but there are no rapids or major obstacles of concern, other than possible blowdowns. In dry season you may encounter riffles over gravel bars, but for the most part you need only to steer around the bends. When you reach the first cottage on the left and the river widens into a marshy area with many water lilies and frequently ducks or herons, you are nearing an old railroad abutment. The right shore here is part of the state's Black Farm Management Area, but leaving the river for a look at the forest trails is not easy.

Beyond the high stone abutment is the pond created by the Woodville dam. It is a narrow pond, as millponds go, and paddling across it seldom involves the wind-bucking effort of other ponds. As you near the dam and bridge, veer to the right for take-out on a narrow path. You'll

Mountain laurel blossoms await canoeists in June.

have to carry your canoe up this path to the road, then across the bridge. In April, at the start of trout season, this bridge is one of the busiest places in the state for fishermen. Before relaunching you may want to look over the dam and what is left of the Woodville Canal that formerly left the river at the right end of the dam. Later, after returning to the river, you will pass the spot where the canal water was returned to the Wood.

Some people relaunch over a guardrail at the end of the bridge; others carry around the bend in the road for an easier access point several yards beyond. It's your choice: shorter or easier. The water below the dam is frequently fast but seldom unmanageable, and it soon flattens out. Less than ½ mile from the bridge you reach what appears to be a fork in the river. Make the sharp turn to the left; the other leg, which has fooled many canoeists, is the emptying end of the old canal. A paddle up it deadends at private property.

The trip from Woodville to Alton Pond, little more than an hour's paddle, is exceptionally easy and scenic. The river is wider here than upstream, with few blowdowns, and the shores are magnificent with not only laurel thickets but also dense pine groves and open marshes. Take time to check out the wildlife; you are likely to see kingbirds, yellow warblers, orioles, catbirds, red-winged blackbirds, kingfishers, herons, and perhaps ospreys. Mammals are harder to predict, but I've encountered otters, muskrats, deer, squirrels, and chipmunks here. Once, a star-nosed mole swam across the river in front of my canoe.

In this area you also are approaching the two best laurel thickets on the river. Twice, where the river bends to the right, you will see immense stands of laurel on the slopes on the left shore. The dazzling pink and white blossoms tower high above you and come right down to the water. Paddling over to them for a rest break is very hard to resist.

You may need the rest, too, once you round a point and enter wide-open Alton Pond. Frequently, a headwind blows directly across the pond, particularly in the afternoons. Staying along the shore may help avoid some of the wind, but the pond is so shallow you may be forced to follow the main channel. Aim for the right end of the bridge. The dam is just before the bridge, and a concrete ramp leading to your car is just before the dam.

19
Pawcatuck River

Alton to Potter Hill

Put-in Point	Take-out Points	Approximate Distance	Approximate Trip Time	Condition of Water	Portages
Alton Dam	Bradford landing	5 miles	2½ hours	Smooth	None
Alton Dam	RI 3 bridge	11½ miles	4½–5 hours	Smooth	Bradford Dam
Alton Dam	Potter Hill Dam	12¾ miles	5–5½ hours	Smooth	Bradford Dam

The Pawcatuck River in southwestern Rhode Island is for those who like their canoeing nice and easy. Flowing through attractive woodlands, the river is smooth and wide, with enough water for late-summer and autumn trips. Because it holds its water well, and because the shoreline trees put on a dazzling foliage display in fall, the Pawcatuck should be saved for late-season canoeing. Pick a day when a slow and leisurely cruise is appealing, for there is little current here except during spring. Hurrying through these woods, with the trees ablaze with color, would be a shame anyway.

The lone exception to the generally quiet waters is a short stretch soon after you begin, where there is a broken dam that sometimes can be run. In addition, there is one portage on the route, a short carry around another dam. The rest of the way is smooth paddling.

A bonus for wildlife watchers: Ospreys have recently begun nesting along the river in both its upper stretch and the lower segment.

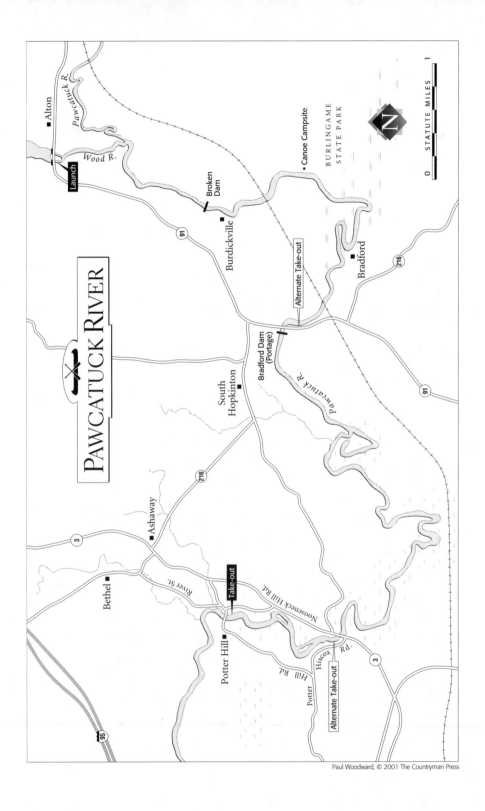

PAWCATUCK RIVER

Alton

Pawcatuck R.

Wood R.

Launch

Broken Dam

Burdickville

91

Canoe Campsite

BURLINGAME STATE PARK

Alternate Take-out

Bradford

216

South Hopkinton

Bradford Dam (Portage)

Pawcatuck R.

91

Ashaway

216

3

Bethel

River St.

Nooseneck Hill Rd.

Take-out

Potter Hill

Potter Hill Rd.

Hiscox Rd.

Alternate Take-out

3

95

N

0   STATUTE MILES   1

Paul Woodward, © 2001 The Countryman Press

Access

You can make a short trip (5 miles, 2½ hours) or a long trip (12¾ miles, 5 to 5½ hours) on the Pawcatuck. The longer run ends by a dam at Potter Hill a short distance north of Westerly. The take-out point is most easily reached by driving to the village of Ashaway on RI 3, turning west on RI 216 and shortly turning south on River Street. Follow River Street to the first bridge, which is just above the Potter Hill Dam. You can park just beyond the bridge beside the burned-out rubble of an old mill. If desired, you can cut a mile off the trip by taking out at the RI 3 bridge; park along Hiscox Road.

The shorter trip, with a take-out at Bradford, includes the faster water near the put-in at Alton and the broken dam run, but avoids the Bradford Dam portage. A state landing on RI 216 in Bradford makes a handy take-out if the 5-mile trip appeals to you.

To reach the put-in point, drive RI 216 (east from Ashaway, north from Bradford) to RI 91, which you will then follow north to Alton. Park in a lot at a state landing beside Alton Dam, and launch your canoe by carrying it across the highway and down a steep bank to the river below the dam. This is actually the Wood River (see Trips 17 and 18) here. A short distance below the dam the Wood joins the Charles River to form the Pawcatuck.

The River

Just below Alton Dam, the Wood River has some current and is very shallow, but it soon opens into a smooth waterway. The Wood runs about ½ mile to its junction with the Charles, which comes in from the left. The combined waters assure you of easy floating the rest of the way. In very early spring, after heavy rains or sudden thaws, the section of the Pawcatuck just below the junction can be wild, but during summer and fall it is pleasant and sets the mood for the rest of the trip: nice and easy.

Both banks are wooded through this first stretch. You will pass a string of houses on the right, each home with its own dock. On the docks are metal benches, showing that the landowners here appreciate the relaxed mood of the river. In fall you will see perhaps the best of the trip's foliage show in this area. Maple trees dominate the shorelines, creating an awesome display of orange, scarlet, and gold. Numerous pines are scattered about, too, and a wide variety of other trees and bushes will be noticed by canoeists who take their time paddling by.

As you reach the first crossing of a power line, look to the left. An osprey nest has been built upon a high pole erected for just this purpose. If you canoe here in late spring or summer, you are likely to see these big fish-eating hawks. When the shoreline vegetation on the left breaks open and reveals a large farm, you are nearing the community of Burdickville and the broken dam. When the current is slow you can safely paddle quite close to the jumbled stones of the dam for a look before going over. The easiest place to run it is at the extreme right, next to a retaining wall, or just to the left of the original right end. In most water conditions, you will run the short rapid rather easily. Experienced canoeists also can run other sections of the original dam but getting out for a lookover is difficult. For those who would rather not attempt the run, simply paddle up to the left side of the dam and lift your canoe over it.

From the broken dam to Bradford you will paddle through a few miles of nearly unbroken woodland. You leave Burdickville heading south and will reach Bradford paddling north, for the river makes a big horseshoe-shaped curve. You will pass under a railroad bridge along one arm of the horseshoe and then later float beneath another bridge of the same railroad. There are no other bridges in this area, which is generally lowland. Shortly after passing the first railroad bridge, at a sweeping right bend, you will come to a well-worn sandy spot at the water's edge on the left. A path to the woods indicates much traffic in and out of the river. This spot is a canoe campsite in Burlingame State Park. Burlingame is Rhode Island's largest campground, with more than 750 tent and trailer campsites, but this is the only area set aside for canoeists. It consists of just rock-ringed fire pits and enough room beneath the tall pines for tents, but it is a pretty spot for a rest break even on day trips.

You are likely to have company along this stretch of the river. Tree

Some Pawcatuck canoeists run the broken dam at Burdickville.

swallows and barn swallows swoop low over the water in pursuit of in-sects throughout the warmer months, and kingfishers will travel with you, screaming in protest, as they fly just ahead of the canoe for con-siderable distances. Fishermen, too, work this area, and you are likely to pass a number of small boats and anchored canoes as you near Brad-ford. If you are taking out at Bradford, start looking for the landing on the left soon after you float under the second railroad bridge.

To continue to Potter Hill, paddle past the Bradford landing and under the RI 91 bridge to the Bradford Dam, which lies shortly beyond. The portage around the right end of the dam and a fish ladder is short and easy. Don't try running this dam; the drop is several feet onto jagged rocks, and few canoes or their passengers are likely to come through undamaged. Below Bradford Dam the river is more murky but winds through lovely wild country, passing woods with tall trees, occa-sional swampy sections, and many acres of tangled marsh vegetation.

It is not uncommon to see deer in the wooded areas. And ducks flock to the patches of swamp in the fall, accounting for the shooting blinds you pass. Before reaching the marshlands you will come upon the stone abutments of a long-vanished bridge where the water is slightly faster. The right side, grassy and shady, offers a perfect picnic site.

As you enter an open, swampy area crossed by power lines, look to the right for an osprey nest on a utility pole. More osprey nests are balanced on other poles farther from the water. There is practically no current through the swamp. Thus it will take a good deal of paddling to reach the next landmark, the RI 3 bridge. If you chose to take out here, your car will be on the left. Once past this bridge, it is about a mile, through a stretch with houses on both shores, to the bridge above Potter Hill Dam. The take-out is best on the right, just before the bridge.

PART III
Connecticut

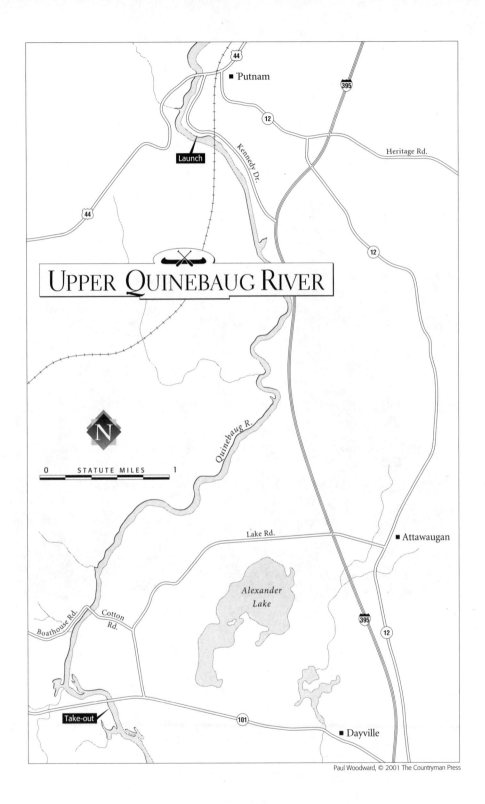

UPPER QUINEBAUG RIVER

■ Putnam

44

395

12

Heritage Rd.

Kennedy Dr.

Launch

44

12

N

0   STATUTE MILES   1

Quinebaug R.

Lake Rd.

■ Attawaugan

Alexander Lake

395

12

Boathouse Rd.

Cotton Rd.

101

Take-out

■ Dayville

20

Upper Quinebaug River

Putnam to north of Danielson

Put-in Point	Take-out Point	Approximate Distance	Approximate Trip Time	Condition of Water	Portages
Simonzi Park, Putnam	CT 101 bridge	6 miles	3 hours	Mostly smooth, some riffles	None

This section of the Quinebaug River in eastern Connecticut is for those who want a few hours of easy paddling and floating. It offers a portage-free trip of 6 miles, with the option of adding several more miles if you want to go beyond the recommended take-out point and then paddle back upriver. With a slow current, that is virtually always possible.

There are a couple of drawbacks to this trip. Unlike the lower Quinebaug (Trip 21), this part of the river runs through less-than-wild surroundings and you are likely to be accompanied by traffic noises in some areas, particularly where I-395 follows the left shore. Still, the banks are forested, there are no homes seen from the river until near the end, and the water level usually remains canoeable even during dry spells. Also, you should see many birds, muskrats, turtles, and other wild creatures.

The ambitious can continue canoeing beyond the take-out at the CT 101 bridge all the way to Danielson, another 6 miles or so, if they wish. But that entire distance is flatwater and there is one dam to negotiate. Because of all the flatwater, and because taking out in Danielson is difficult, the CT 101 bridge is suggested as a terminus for this trip.

Access

Drive CT 101 west of Dayville to the river; a lane on the south side leads to a parking area and your take-out.

To reach the put-in, follow CT 101 east about 2½ miles to CT 12, just beyond the I-395 interchange. Go left on CT 12 about 6 miles to Putnam, turn left on US 44, and after a short distance you will reach Kennedy Drive at the river. Take a left onto Kennedy Drive and look for the THIRD parking area in a riverside picnic ground called the John F. Simonzi Sr. Memorial Park. At the far end of the park is a designated canoe launching area.

The River

You will carry your canoe across a bike path to reach the river, and as soon as you launch you will pass under a bridge that carries bicyclists across the water. Here, the river is likely to be fairly fast and riffly, especially in low water. Not far beyond the bridge the water flattens out and you reach an island. There will be more islands ahead, just as there will be more riffles.

After floating beneath a second bridge you reach a good section of the trip with tall trees flanking the water and considerable wildlife. We've encountered numerous herons, ospreys, ducks, geese, kingfishers, songbirds, and muskrats here, and on one summer trip we watched two deer stroll across the river on a gravel bar. Even when you near I-395 and can hear the traffic, your view will be mostly of the forested banks. With numerous oaks, this segment is particularly attractive in late autumn, when the oaks turn red, maroon, and golden brown.

There is more wildlife ahead. In several places the banks tower high; look for the tunnel nests of kingfishers. You should also see gnawed trees that indicate the presence of beavers. Numerous animal trails lead through the woods and weeds down to the water, and you can find the tracks of deer, raccoons, and other animals in the shoreline mud.

For the most part the water alternates between flat and riffly. One

This bridge now carries bicyclists over the Quinebaug.

patch of large boulders can be an interesting run in high water. Just beyond the boulders, look on the right for the stonework of a long-vanished mill. There are several attractive picnic sites on the right shore, but they are posted; please respect the signs.

The next bridge, normally reached in under 3 hours, signals the end of all riffles and quickwater. Just beyond this bridge you will pass the first home you've seen since your launch, on the right, and there will be a gravel road running along the right. After a few more houses and a few more curves, you reach the green CT 101 bridge that is your take-out. Unless you want to paddle on toward Danielson before turning around, head for the right shore just beyond the bridge.

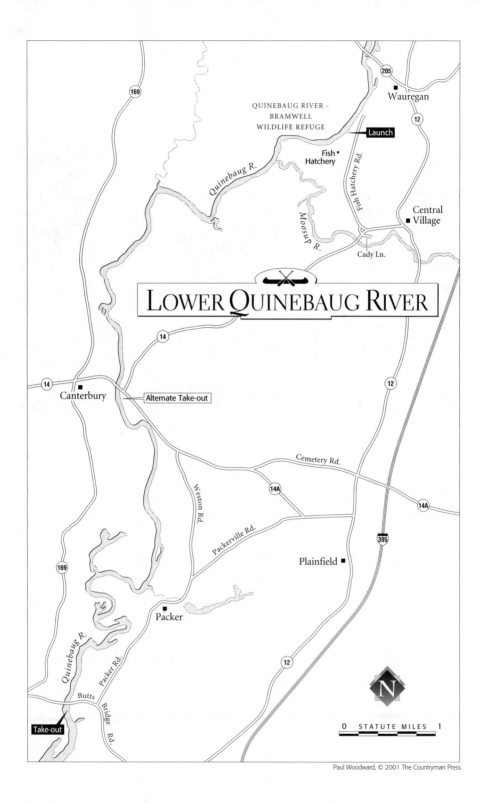

QUINEBAUG RIVER -
BRAMWELL
WILDLIFE REFUGE

Wauregan

205

12

Launch

Fish
Hatchery

Fish Hatchery Rd.

Quinebaug R.

Central
Village

Moosup R.

Cady Ln.

LOWER QUINEBAUG RIVER

14

14

Canterbury

Alternate Take-out

12

Cemetery Rd.

Weston Rd.

14A

14A

Packerville Rd.

395

Plainfield

169

Packer

Quinebaug R.

Packer Rd.

Butts

Bridge Rd.

Take-out

12

N

0   STATUTE MILES   1

Paul Woodward, © 2001 The Countryman Press

21

Lower Quinebaug River

Central Village to north of Jewett City

Put-in Point	Take-out Points	Approximate Distance	Approximate Trip Time	Condition of Water	Portages
Fish Hatchery Road	CT 14 bridge	5 1/2 miles	2 hours	Mostly smooth	None
Fish Hatchery Road	Butts Bridge Road bridge	10 1/2 miles	4–4 1/2 hours	Mostly smooth	None

Save the Quinebaug River for a day in midspring, after whitewater fever has subsided but before New England rivers slow to their summer pace. On a sparkling day in May or early June the Quinebaug offers an easy cruise through an underrated area rich in both wildlife and scenic attractions.

The Quinebaug flows down the eastern edge of Connecticut until it joins the Shetucket (see Trip 23) just above Norwich to form the Thames. Many upper reaches of the Quinebaug have long been harnessed for power, and numerous dams make canoeing much of that area difficult, although one other segment (see Trip 20) is also included in this book. In the stretch described here, you can enjoy a most pleasant 10 1/2-mile float without a single portage. There are brief sections of quickwater shortly after the put-in, but most of the trip is a smooth journey. In summer or low water, you may find the going a bit scratchy in places. Usually, the current is fast enough to require little paddling, yet calm enough to allow time to enjoy the surroundings.

The Quinebaug is wide enough for maneuvering around rocks.

Access

You have a choice of take-out points. You can end your trip at the CT 14 bridge a few miles west of Central Village, giving you a short journey of approximately 5½ miles that will last 2½ hours or less. This section includes the most attractive scenery along the river and runs through a wildlife management area. The take-out is at River Park, just beyond the CT 14 bridge.

If you prefer a longer trip, continue driving west on CT 14 to CT 169, turn left (south), and go about 4 miles to Butts Bridge Road. A left turn here and a short drive will take you back to the river. The take-out is on the left bank, so cross the bridge and continue to the end of the guardrail, where you can find adequate parking space. Canoeing to this bridge stretches your trip to about 10½ miles and will take about 4 to 4½ hours, longer if you take a lunch break.

To reach the put-in, drive east on CT 14 to the edge of Central

Village, then turn left onto Cady Lane. Continue on this road as it becomes Fish Hatchery Road and drive past the hatchery buildings to a lane that runs to the left down to the river. Hatchery officials allow canoe launching here but ask that vehicles be returned to a designated parking area partway up the lane.

The River

At your start, the river is very shallow and can be scratchy in times of low water. For that reason, and because of the increased activity of birds in spring, May and early June are usually better times for canoeing this river than midsummer. You will notice the beauty of the river immediately. The shores are lovely with huge trees towering above—many hemlocks as well as beeches and pines. In addition, there are numerous magnificent old sycamores and lush thickets of mountain laurel. The blossoms of the laurel add a bonus for canoeists passing this area in late spring.

In less than an hour after launching, you will pass a feeder stream entering quietly from the left. This is the Moosup River, a whitewater stream frequently used by canoeists in March. Here, at its end, it is calm and unpretentious. Many canoeists on the Quinebaug don't even notice it. Nobody will miss the next feature, though, for just past the Moosup junction you come to perhaps the largest patch of rapids on this trip. It is easy to pull out on the right and walk ahead for a good look at the rapids. Carry around on the right, too, if the route appears too difficult or the water is too low. Usually this section can be run without trouble if you stay to the right of center.

After this quickwater, there is smooth sailing most of the rest of the way, interspersed with a few riffles. Take time to enjoy the wildlife. During spring, you may flush wood ducks, mallards, or black ducks at nearly every bend. Kingfishers often protest from perches above you, sandpipers may be probing the shoreline, and herons are often stalking through the shallows. In addition, songbirds maintain a musical din in the woods. And you are likely to see a muskrat or two swim across the river ahead of your canoe.

As you near a sharp left turn in the river, you will hear what sounds like rapids. A number of boulders at the water's edge on the right create the noise but they usually present no problem if you stay to the left as you swing around the bend. There are only a few other areas of minor riffles before you reach the CT 14 bridge, your terminus if you opted for the shorter trip. The take-out is just before the bridge on the right.

Those who continue canoeing to Butts Bridge Road will find even fewer riffles in this stretch. First there is a high, rocky ridge decorated with hemlock and laurel on the right shore, but soon the banks flatten into farm fields, most of which are screened from the river by trees. The Quinebaug then meanders through a broad flood plain. It is interesting to note just how high the shoreline trees are scarred from being struck by ice and debris during the late winter floods. There are no houses along the river here and the scenery, while not as spectacular as along the first part of the trip, remains pleasant except for the few minutes it takes to pass a landfill on the left.

Wildlife is abundant here as well. Crows call from the tall trees, red-winged blackbirds sing from the farm fields, and there are as many ducks here as in the protected area upriver. The high banks, again covered with hemlock and laurel, return, restoring the wilderness atmosphere to the river.

The next bridge, a high steel structure, is the Butts Bridge Road bridge, your take-out point. Go just beyond the bridge and pull out on the left.

22

Hopeville Pond–Pachaug River

Hopeville

Put-in and Take-out Point	Approximate Distance	Approximate Trip Time	Condition of Water	Portages
Hopeville Pond State Park	5½ miles	3–4 hours	Smooth	None

If you find yourself with a few hours and want to go canoeing, but no partners are available or you don't want to use a second vehicle for one-way trips, give Hopeville Pond in eastern Connecticut a try. It offers plenty of relaxed paddling through a state park, then across a narrow pond, and up a woodsy river. When you've paddled to your heart's content, you can easily return to your place of put-in.

The pond resembles a wide river, and that's because it was the Pachaug River before a dam created the pond many years ago. On this paddle you can mosey along one shore of the pond, exploring the coves and backwaters, where considerable wildlife can be found, then take a look at what remains of the Pachaug between dams.

Because of the dams the water level remains high all year. The park where the trip begins is a busy place in summer, though, and an entrance fee is charged at that time. You may want to visit just before Memorial Day or after Labor Day.

Access

Take I-395 to Exit 86, then follow CT 201 east, and watch for the signs for the park. The boat ramp is at the far end of a camping area. After

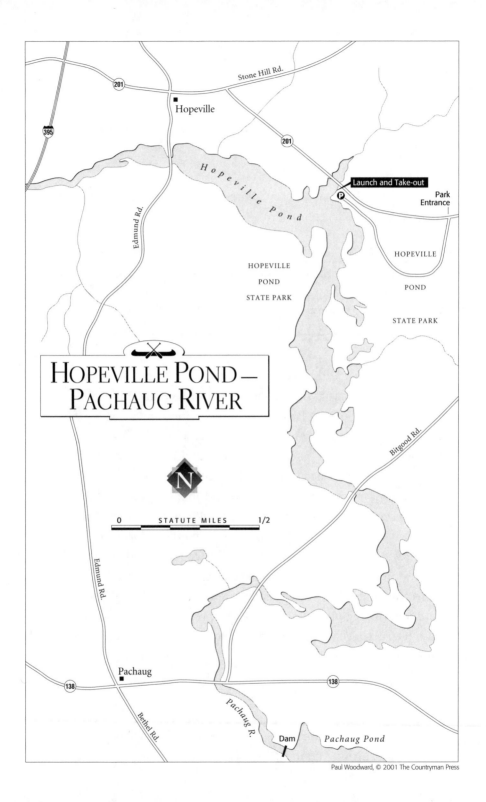

Paul Woodward, © 2001 The Countryman Press

unloading your canoe you may be asked to leave your car at a small parking lot beside a ranger station 100 yards or so back up the road.

The River

Paddle to the left from the ramp channel (going to the right would take you to the pond's dam rather quickly). As you follow the left shore, you'll pass a small swimming area and most of the campsites. Soon you'll go past a cluster of homes and leave the park.

Continue along the shore; your next landmark is a bridge. This bridge, for Bitgood Road, is less than half an hour from your start and apparently is irresistible to barn swallows. If you visit in summer you are likely to see a dozen nests plastered underneath, often just a foot or two above your head. The adult birds will be swooping around the bridge and pond, tending their young and snatching insects from the air. They put on quite a show.

Beyond the bridge, the pond takes on a different, more pastoral look with fewer homes, some farmland beyond the shoreline trees, and coves filled with water lilies, turtles, herons, ducks, and muskrats. You are also likely to find bass fishermen here, particularly if you come on a summer weekend; the coves are known to harbor some impressive fish.

One cattle farm can be seen above the left bank; I think it adds to the charm of the place. Below the farm, where the river-pond makes a sweeping bend to the right, is an abandoned beaver lodge. On one visit, when I paddled up to examine the lodge, I found a 4-foot-long black snake sunning itself on the mound. Around the bend, the main channel begins narrowing, although there are more coves, and soon you will find yourself out of the pond altogether and on a river. Here you should notice beaver signs—gnawed stumps and branches—along with numerous songbirds and waterbirds.

In this stretch you pass under a second bridge (also for Bitgood Road) and then paddle through a narrow segment in which you can see an active beaver lodge on the right shore. You may have to look carefully; it's screened by trees and bushes. This is the "old" Pachaug River with tall trees. The most impressive tree, perhaps, can be found just as

Shallow coves are decorated with water lilies.

you approach the next bridge. It is a magnificent sycamore on the right bank, on the grounds of a church.

This third bridge, for CT 138 in the village of Griswold, is usually my turnaround point. You could paddle another ¼ mile or so to the next dam, which holds back the larger and more developed Pachaug Pond, but I prefer making the turn here and floating back into Hopeville Pond. Usually, there are baby ducks or orioles or something else worth seeing on the return trip that I missed on the way in.

23

Shetucket River

South Windham to Baltic

Put-in Point	Take-out Point	Approximate Distance	Approximate Trip Time	Condition of Water	Portages
CT 203 bridge	CT 97 bridge	7¾ miles	3–3½ hours	Smooth early, then riffles	Scotland Dam

In eastern Connecticut, canoeists seeking whitewater usually head for the Salmon River (see Trip 25), while those preferring flatwater go to the Quinebaug (see Trips 20 and 21). Not as well known, perhaps, but located in the same general area, is the Shetucket River; it offers both kinds of water.

The quickwater is usually more on the order of riffles than rapids, but under the right conditions it provides a taste of what rock-dodging is all about. There are no dangerous spots, just scattered patches of boulders with plenty of room to maneuver your canoe. The flatwater segment of this trip—the first 3 miles or so—is almost mirror smooth. Family groups and less experienced canoeists should be able to handle this journey with little difficulty. As with all rivers, however, the Shetucket's conditions can fluctuate with water levels, so some caution should be taken after heavy rains and sudden thaws.

What splits the Shetucket into virtually two separate rivers is the huge Scotland Dam. The dam must be portaged, but the carry, although long, is not particularly difficult and it is the only one on this trip. The total distance of the trip is about 7¾ miles; normally it will take about 3½ hours. A strong headwind in the pondlike stretch above the dam or extremely low water with lots of bottom-scraping below the

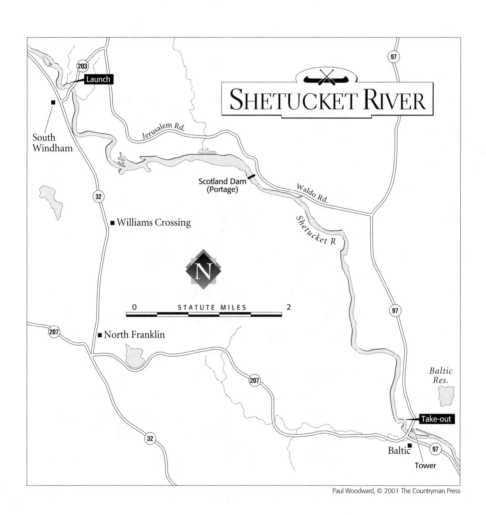

SHETUCKET RIVER

97

203

Launch

Jerusalem Rd.

South
Windham

Scotland Dam
(Portage)

Waldo Rd.

32

Shetucket R

■ Williams Crossing

N

0   STATUTE MILES   2

97

207

■ North Franklin

207

Baltic
Res.

32

Take-out

Baltic

97

Tower

Paul Woodward, © 2001 The Countryman Press

dam, however, will slow you down considerably. Both factors should be considered before starting out.

Access

The put-in is at the CT 203 bridge at the village of South Windham, just downriver from Willimantic. You will take out at the CT 97 bridge in Baltic. Access is not particularly easy at either end. Be prepared to carry your canoe and gear a few yards up or down steeper slopes than on most of the trips described in this book.

At Baltic, drive to a large parking area just east of the bridge and leave your car in the extreme right corner of the lot. The best take-out is down a path to the right. It is possible to take out closer to your car, but if you do you will have to cope with a stronger current and then climb a steep, stony bank.

To reach the put-in, pick up CT 207 just west of the bridge at take-out, follow it west 5 miles to North Franklin, then take CT 32 north 3 miles to CT 203. The bridge over the Shetucket is a short distance to your right on CT 203. A slower route to the put-in is suggested if you want a look at the river conditions before you start. By taking CT 97 north from Baltic and turning left onto Waldo Road, you can go past Scotland Dam. After seeing how much water is flowing through the dam, continue on the curvy road, now Jerusalem Road, north to CT 203, then turn left and drive to the river.

There is steep lane down to the water just east of the CT 203 bridge, but the lane is often badly eroded and you may not want to chance getting stuck. Ample parking is available farther east at an electric power plant, but your canoe may have to be carried down the lane to the water.

The River

Once on the river, you are likely to forget the problems you met in launching. There is some current in this area, but the river is wide and smooth, except for one spot that sometimes offers riffles. Dense stands of hemlocks contrast pleasantly with the lighter green of birches,

Anglers can often be seen on the Shetucket near Baltic.

maples, beeches, and oaks. Ferns, laurel, and other undergrowth are abundant, and at times moss-covered ledges rise above the shorelines. The forest is virtually unbroken all the way to the dam.

If there is a headwind, paddle close to shore. The right bank offers the most protection and also has the better scenery. After a few bends and as the river grows wider, you will notice some landmarks on the left shore—a picnic pavilion, a dock, railroad tracks, and later a few cottages perched at the water's edge. When you pass the cottages you are nearing the Scotland Dam, so stay along the right shore. You will see a brick maintenance building at the left end of the dam as you round a bend. If you are already floating along the right bank, you should have no problem in easing up to the right end. This dam is one of the more elaborate of those canoeists encounter in southern New England. It is controlled by computers that calculate power requirements, so the amount of water it releases varies considerably.

Reentering the river requires a carry across the dike at the dam's right end, then down a lane to a mass of rocks. You can launch here in a quiet eddy and then take a good look back at the dam, now towering above you, before swinging out into the current. Even with the increased current, the river remains quite smooth for $\frac{1}{4}$ mile or so. Then, just as you pass a feeder stream coming in from the left, you reach the riffles. Water depth determines the number of rocks you can float over and those that must be avoided, but slipping past these obstacles is usually easy and fun. The current is good—normally you can float the $4\frac{1}{2}$ miles from the Scotland Dam to Baltic in about $1\frac{1}{2}$ to 2 hours. This stretch is a delightful change of pace after the flatwater earlier in the trip. The river remains wide, and rocks and riffles combine with wooded banks to create a feeling that you are in a wilderness setting rather than midway between the cities of Willimantic and Norwich.

Soon after passing a cabin in a clearing on the right, the river makes a sweeping curve to the right. Stay along the right shore to remain in the best channel. The left side is very shallow. For some distance here, brief periods of calm water alternate with long stretches of "bumpy" water—that is, minor riffles and good, fast current. You will reach one section in which large boulders are strewn across the river. It looks difficult from a distance, but there is plenty of room for you to float by.

After passing a large squarish rock in midriver, you will be nearing the final stretch, a lengthy "rock garden" that will involve plenty of maneuvering. When the high stone tower of a mill building looms into view, prepare to move out of the current to the left. The landing spot is on the outside of a curve, just above another set of riffles and the CT 97 bridge.

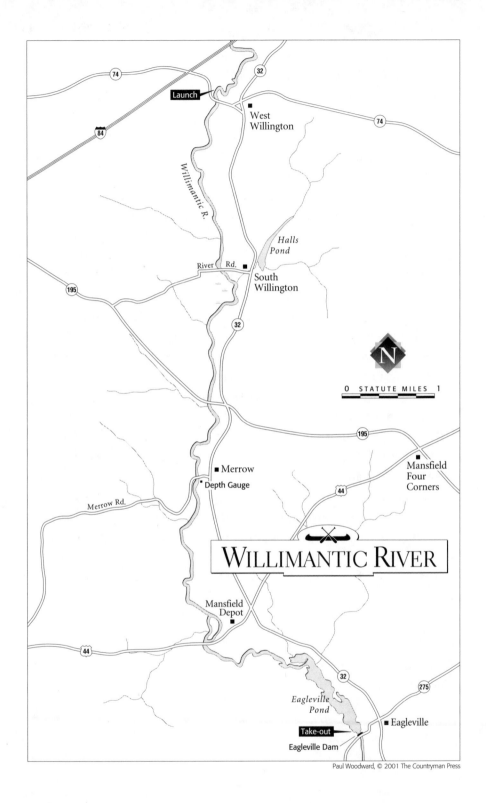

74

32

Launch

84

West
Willington

74

Willimantic R.

*Halls
Pond*

River Rd.

South
Willington

195

32

N

0 STATUTE MILES 1

195

Merrow

Mansfield
Four
Corners

Depth Gauge

44

Merrow Rd.

WILLIMANTIC RIVER

Mansfield
Depot

44

32

275

*Eagleville
Pond*

Eagleville

Take-out

Eagleville Dam

24

Willimantic River

West Willington to Eagleville

Put-in Point	Take-out Point	Approximate Distance	Approximate Trip Time	Condition of Water	Portages
CT 74 bridge	Eagleville Dam	10 miles	3–3½ hours	Mostly fast until near end	None

The Willimantic River east of Hartford is ideal for canoeists who want to try quickwater for the first time, or perhaps brush up their rock-dodging skills before tackling some of the wilder rivers of New England. This stretch of the Willimantic offers approximately 10 miles of delightful floating through a scenic, wooded valley. The river, a personal favorite, is known for its natural beauty, its fishing, and its rocks. For most of this trip you won't have much time to admire the leafy shorelines; you'll be too busy steering your way around rocks in the stream and trying to read the next batch of riffles. The water is shallow virtually all the way, and about the only danger is the possibility of scratching or maybe denting your canoe.

As with most shallow rivers, you'll need adequate depth to avoid getting hung up on rocks and gravel bars. Fortunately, the Willimantic has a gauge you can check before launching. It is beneath a bridge on Merrow Road off CT 32 between CT 195 and US 44 in the town of Mansfield. A reading of 2.1 is recommended for good canoeing, although I've done the river at 1.8 with only minor bottom-scraping.

Access

The most popular run on the Willimantic is from near Stafford Springs to Eagleville Dam, a distance of more than 14 miles. However, I suggest cutting off the first few miles, which tend to be quite shallow and scratchy, and putting in at Nye-Holman State Forest just off CT 74 in West Willington.

To leave a car at the take-out, drive CT 32 to Eagleville, which is about 6 miles north of the city of Willimantic, and turn west on CT 275. There is parking space on both ends of the dam, but the easier take-out is on the west side of the dam, so cross the river.

In driving to the put-in point, follow CT 32 north until reaching CT 74 at West Willington, then turn left, cross the river, and pull into the state forest on the right. Go about 100 yards down the entrance road to a short lane on the right.

If you want to put in farther upriver, stay on CT 32 until it crosses the river 2½ miles beyond the I-84 overpass. Take the first left, Plains Road, a short distance to a small launch site on the left.

The River

At the start, whether entering at Plains Road or Nye-Holman, the river is narrow, flat, and loud, gurgling over thousands of rocks. These conditions are a good indication of what lies ahead, for although the river widens as it flows south, these little rapids continue until you reach the deadwater above Eagleville Dam. A look at the larger rocks in the water shows just how popular this river is with canoeists. Nearly every stone carries scrape marks—red, green, or yellow paint, or the white scars left by aluminum canoes. But even this upper portion can be canoed with some care and skill. You may occasionally nudge a submerged rock unseen in the water, but for the most part winding your way through the maze is not only possible but very enjoyable. If you do run aground, it's usually a simple matter for the stern person to step into the water and float the canoe a few feet to deeper water.

For much of the early paddling, stretches of riffles alternate with calm periods. In the smooth stretches you can take in the hemlocks, birches, laurel, and maples that decorate the river's banks, effectively screening you from nearly all houses and roadways. But don't be fooled into thinking the riffles are finished. After each brief respite you will

Calm stretches between riffles give you time to look around.

come to many more, some of which are punctuated by big boulders scattered haphazardly across the river. There is, however, usually enough water to make the maneuvering easy and fun.

You may want to stop in this area and try the fishing. The upper Willimantic is heavily stocked with trout; you are likely to meet fishermen here on any spring trip. Only fly-fishing is permitted and all fish caught must be released. The river runs through a valley, and breaks in the shoreline foliage reveal lush farmlands. One minute you'll feel far removed from all civilization, alone with the birdsong and tumbling river, and the next you will be treated to the aroma of new-mown hay or find yourself being stared at by a herd of cattle.

Although there are no homes on the shores, you will pass under several bridges. After floating under CT 195 (the third bridge if you launched in West Willington), you begin to see signs of beavers, which have moved into the river system in recent years. Trunks of trees along the shores have been gnawed near the ground, and you are likely to run across at least a beaver dam or two. Unless the water is very low, you can usually go over the dams. It is at the fourth bridge from West Willington that you will find the water-level gauge—look for steps coming down to the water on the left—and a pleasant little park, a good spot for a lunch break.

Throughout the trip you are likely to see birds: kingfishers, herons, ducks, songbirds. We once saw a large owl fly off and an osprey fishing for trout. Once you pass beneath a blue bridge, you are approaching the deadwater of Eagleville Lake. Despite its name, it is not particularly wide and can be a pleasant paddle if there is no headwind. Frequently you'll see many birds here, too, along with thick growths of water lilies and pickerelweed.

If you parked at the west end of the dam, follow the right shore of the lake. After paddling through an open, marshy segment, you'll begin seeing homes on the bank and will pass a picturesque cottage on a small island before reaching your take-out. Like the rest of the Willimantic, the cottage can make you pause in admiration. You may wish you could come to this river more often.

25

Salmon River

West of Colchester to near Westchester

Put-in Point	Take-out Point	Approximate Distance	Approximate Trip Time	Condition of Water	Portages
River Road bridge	Old Comstock Bridge	3½ miles	2–2½ hours	Rapids and riffles	One or none

For many canoeists in southern New England, spring would not be complete without a run on the Salmon River in south-central Connecticut. Traffic on the Salmon can be heavy in late March and early April, as whitewater enthusiasts swarm in from Hartford and the University of Connecticut to the north, Rhode Island to the east, and the New York City area to the southwest. Not many leave the Salmon disappointed.

The Salmon is definitely a whitewater river. It consists of almost continuous rapids and should not be attempted by novices unless accompanied by experienced canoeists. Even the very best canoeists should keep safety uppermost in mind. Go in a group, take extra paddles, wear a life jacket, and if at all possible wear a wetsuit—the water is extremely cold in March. It is a rare canoeist indeed who can negotiate all the maneuvers and obstacles on this stretch of river without getting wet.

Several segments of the Salmon and the two smaller rivers that form it, the Blackledge and the Jeremy, can be canoed, but the section described here is probably the most popular. This is a short stretch, barely 3½ miles long, but it is 3½ miles of quickwater and rapids rated mostly Class II by the American Canoe Association and the Appalachian Mountain Club. In moderately high water there are no portages except, perhaps, for a broken dam near the end. And even the

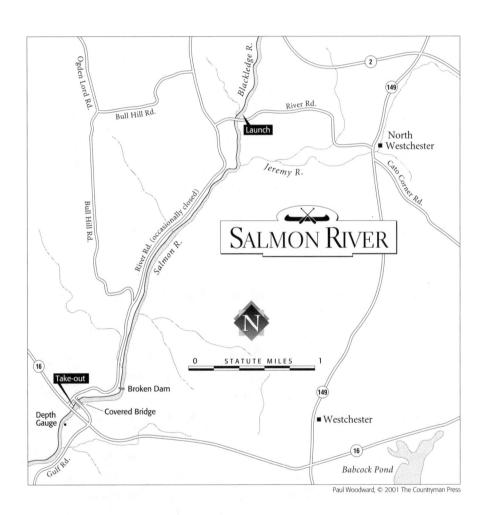

Ogden Lord Rd.

Blackledge R.

2

149

Bull Hill Rd.

River Rd.

Launch

North
Westchester

Cato Corner Rd.

Jeremy R.

Bull Hill Rd.

River Rd. (occasionally closed)

Salmon R.

⚓ ⚓

SALMON RIVER

N

0   STATUTE MILES   1

16

Take-out

Broken Dam

149

Depth
Gauge

Covered Bridge

Westchester

Gulf Rd.

16

Babcock Pond

Paul Woodward, © 2001 The Countryman Press

dam can be run by the more adventurous. In fact, for many it is the highlight of the trip.

Water depth, the key in any whitewater canoeing, is especially critical on the Salmon, where the rapids and their degree of difficulty change constantly. One rainstorm, for example, can mean the difference between an exhilarating dash down the river and a day spent scratching bottom on a thousand rocks. Fortunately, there is a water gauge you can check before entering the river; it should indicate whether there is enough water for good canoeing. The gauge is just below your take-out point.

When planning your trip, keep in mind that the river runs through the Salmon River Trout Management Area and that the waterway is very popular with anglers. Go before fishing season, which usually begins the third Saturday in April, and you can avoid having to compete with people standing in the very channels you want to run.

Access

The best route to the take-out is CT 2 to Exit 16 a few miles west of Colchester. That exit puts you on CT 149, which you then follow south to CT 16 in Westchester. Turn right and drive 2 miles to the river. Just upstream from the CT 16 bridge is a picturesque wooden covered bridge called the Old Comstock Bridge. This bridge and a parking area on the far shore make for a convenient take-out. If you have only one or two cars, though, I suggest taking out on the near side of the river, across from the parking lot, virtually under the covered bridge, at the end of Bridge Street. Take-out is easier here, but parking is better on the far, or western, side of the river.

Look over the water's depth at the covered bridge; this is one of the most shallow segments of the trip. If the water flowing over the countless rocks between the covered bridge and the CT 16 bridge appears deep enough for a canoe, chances are there will be enough water for running the rapids upstream. If many of these rocks are exposed, you may be spending as much time dragging the canoe as paddling it. Some canoeists use an iron ring in the downstream side of the right abutment of the covered bridge as an indicator. If the ring is less than 2 feet above the water, the river is passable. For a more definitive reading, walk about 50 yards downstream from the CT 16 bridge, on the left, or eastern, shore, and look for a wooden gauge attached to a pipe. It's not easy to find and the bank is steep, but the gauge shows the water depth. A reading of 4 feet means there is enough water to ride the rapids.

To reach the put-in on the Blackledge River just above the beginning of the Salmon proper, you have some choices. You can follow Bull Hill Road, which runs by the covered bridge, on its roundabout way north to River Road, or you can take a dirt road that branches off to the right from Bull Hill Road and follows the river. Unfortunately, the dirt road, which runs through Salmon River State Forest and provides great views of the rapids, is usually not open until fishing season, which begins later than many canoeists want to run the river. You can also reach River Road by retracing your route on CT 16 and CT 149. The best put-in is on the upstream side of the east end of the River Road bridge.

The River

The Blackledge here is quite shallow for the first $\frac{1}{2}$ mile or so. Almost immediately after passing under the River Road bridge, you reach an island; the left passage is usually better. Then you pass under an old railroad bridge that now is part of a bike path. When a second stream, the Jeremy, comes in from the left, you will be on the Salmon. Here, both the rapids and the fun begin.

Big boulders dot the riverbed, and hundreds of other rocks lurk at or near the surface. You will find yourself hurtling through a spectacular valley whose walls are blanketed with hemlocks, but don't spend too much time looking around. Keep your eyes on the rocks and be prepared to do a lot of back-watering, drawing, and sweeping. Veteran canoeists say you cannot think about dodging the rocks one at a time; you have to think three of four maneuvers ahead. If you don't, you just might make a terrific move around one set of boulders and find yourself broadside to the next one.

The time estimate given for this trip, 2 to $2\frac{1}{2}$ hours, can be reduced

Always look over this broken dam chute before trying to go through it.

by making a straight, continuous run. Most canoeists do this river in groups, however, and it is a common practice for group leaders to pull over to shore or into an eddy after each patch of rapids to make certain all the other canoes have made the run successfully. This is a good safety procedure. It would be a mistake anyway to hurry through the Salmon River experience. It is better to savor the fun.

A landmark to look for is a fishing-access spot for the handicapped on the right bank. Two ramps enable wheelchair-bound anglers to try their luck at the river's trout and salmon. Some canoeists and kayakers take out here, but it's a rather long carry up the ramps and across the road to the parking area. And taking out here would make you miss both the broken-dam excitement and the covered bridge.

About ¼ mile beyond the ramps for the handicapped, and heard before seen, are the washed-out dam and the foaming, frothing falls over the ledge rocks that remain. A high stone foundation on the right shore still clearly marks the spot. It is wise to pull out and walk ahead for a good look at what is in store. If you doubt your canoeing or swimming ability, carry around this falls. No momentary thrill is worth risking a tragedy. The falls can be run, however, through a deep chute that cuts through the ledge at the extreme right, just below your scouting position on the foundation. Once through the chute, you will drop into a pool and then you must make a quick left turn over a much smaller falls. If you take in a lot of water in the chute, just pull over to the right bank and empty your canoe before leaving the pool.

But don't forget to look over the falls before trying it. Once, while we were scouting the chute, two canoes approached carrying young couples who obviously had no intention of pulling ashore. They simply ignored our calls. The first, luckily, slipped over the falls successfully. The second one swamped. The canoe went down, and the two occupants got soaked. They were wearing neither life preservers nor wetsuits, and they had to be helped from the icy water. It's likely they will show a bit more respect for the falls the next time around.

After the broken-dam falls, there are several stretches of riffles and a ledge or two on which heavily loaded canoes can get hung up. In less than $\frac{1}{2}$ mile, however, you will come to the covered bridge and your take-out.

26

Lower Farmington River

Farmington to Weatogue

Put-in Point	Take-out Point	Approximate Distance	Approximate Trip Time	Condition of Water	Portages
CT 4 landing	CT 185 bridge	9½ miles	3½–4 hours	Smooth	None

In most canoeing books, the stretch of the Farmington River running from Farmington to Weatogue, just west of Hartford, is usually covered in one sentence. One guide popular with New England sportsmen dismisses the entire area with 14 words: "Here the river turns north and there is a fair current but no quickwater." It deserves far more attention.

As with the Housatonic River (see Trips 1, 29, and 30), the Farmington offers you a choice. You can go a few miles northwest and do the upper Farmington (see Trip 27) with its rapids, rocky riffles, trout pools, and forested shorelines. Or you can stay closer to Hartford and do the lower Farmington, a relaxing 9½-mile float through an attractive valley. Along this portion of the river you'll see a surprisingly large variety of wildlife, pass by several golf courses and extensive farm fields, enjoy views of Talcott Mountain and Heublein Tower, look for King Philip's Cave high on a ridge above the river, and finally take out beside one of the largest and most impressive trees in Connecticut.

This trip is ideal for family groups, as there are no portages, rapids, or obstacles of any kind. And unlike the upper Farmington, which runs too shallow during the summer and fall for pleasant canoeing, this stretch can usually be run throughout the year.

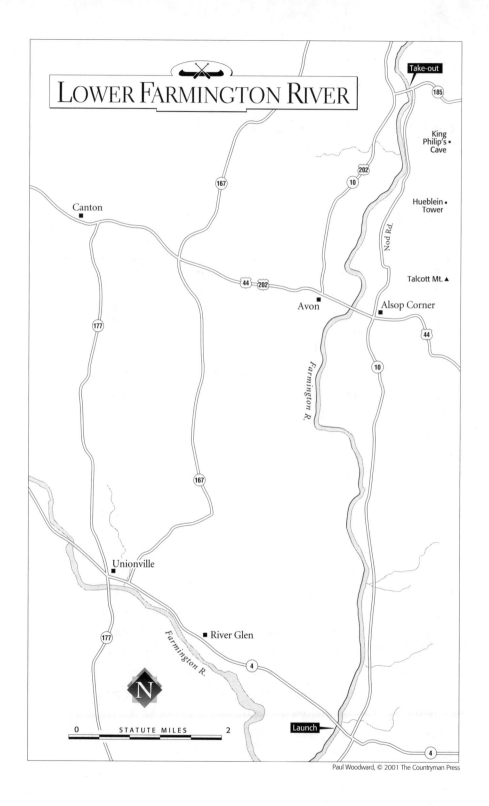

LOWER FARMINGTON RIVER

Take-out

185

King Philip's Cave ■

202

10

Hueblein Tower ■

167

Nod Rd.

Canton ■

Talcott Mt. ▲

177

44 202

Avon ■

Alsop Corner ■

44

10

167

Farmington R.

Unionville ■

177

Farmington R.

River Glen ■

4

N

Launch

0   STATUTE MILES   2

4

Paul Woodward, © 2001 The Countryman Press

Access

Access is easy. To leave a car at the take-out, drive on CT 185 to where it crosses the Farmington in the Weatogue section of Simsbury. At the east end of the bridge, Nod Road breaks off to the south; there is a large parking area beside the river just a few yards down this road. For a more aesthetic take-out, however, follow a lane that goes north off CT 185. This lane leads to another large parking area dominated by an immense sycamore tree. A stone marker at its base identifies the tree as the Pinchot Sycamore and reveals its circumference, 23 feet, 7 inches. The tree was named for Gifford Pinchot of Simsbury, who was the first chief of the U.S. Forestry Service.

The put-in is off CT 4 just above the town of Farmington. You can take Nod Road from CT 185 south to Avon, or you can cross the river and follow CT 10–US 202 to Avon, where you bear left onto US 44 briefly and cross the river. Then continue south on CT 10–US 202 until you arrive at CT 4. Go right on CT 4, and immediately after crossing the bridge turn left down a lane to the landing. You'll find plenty of parking room.

The River

This valley is quite heavily settled and industrialized, but you would never know it from traveling on the river. For the most part, large trees line both shores and high banks blot out roads, buildings, and other signs of "civilization." The early going is somewhat typical of the entire trip. Tall maples, sycamores, and oaks shade the wide and smooth river. In addition, you'll notice a liberal sprinkling of mountain laurel, honeysuckle, and dogwood, all easy to spot in spring when they are in bloom. Many of the stately old trees clinging to the banks are undercut. Occasionally, you'll come across trees that have fallen into the water, but the river is so wide there are no problems in swinging around them.

There is a golf course on the right soon after your start, then one on the left. Later, you will pass more golf courses, one shortly before your take-out. The trip, however, is not all golf courses. There are many

This part of the Farmington River is often mirror-smooth and easy to float.

areas of woods. In fact, you'll probably see more wildlife on this trip than on the upper Farmington even though that area more closely resembles what people call "wilderness." There, heavy use by canoeists, fishermen, campers, and hikers scares off many of the animals and birds. In addition, what is there is often overlooked because canoeing quickwater doesn't leave much time for looking around.

Here, however, it is a different matter. Let the current do the work, and enjoy your surroundings. Gray squirrels and chipmunks are abundant along the shorelines. So are orioles, cardinals, and chickadees. Swallows and kingbirds swoop over the water. Sandpipers dance along the mudflats. Kingfishers call from their perches. Woodchucks are often seen waddling along the banks, and muskrats frequently swim ahead of your canoe. Raccoon tracks can be found on any sandbar, and often deer tracks, too. On one May trip on this stretch we even came across two gray fox kits playing outside their den.

You come to the busy US 44 strip in Avon, approximately 6 miles from the starting point, in 2 to 2½ hours. Here, after leaving an extensive golf course behind, you'll come abreast the open fields, many of which formerly grew tobacco, Unfortunately, the high banks—a blessing elsewhere—are a drawback along this stretch because they prevent good views of the farms with their fields and huge drying barns. In many cases all you'll be able to see of the farms from the river are pumps that carry water to the fields. The high banks also make it difficult to find good picnic spots in this area.

Talcott Mountain, however, is high enough to be seen over the banks. It extends along your right for the rest of the journey. The most interesting feature on the ridge is the Heublein Tower, built by the Heublein family of cocktail fame. Long Island Sound can be seen from the tower on a clear day. As you view it from the river, the tower resembles a blunt-nosed rocket poised for takeoff.

Keep an eye on the tower, for just about the time you pull even with it, the river bends to the right and the bow of your canoe will be pointing directly toward a stony knoll at the northern end of the Talcott Mountain ridge. Look closely, and you'll be able to see a rectangular hole. This is the cave from which the Indian chief, King Philip, supposedly directed the burning of Simsbury, just down the river, in 1676. Today the cave overlooks peaceful farms and one more golf course. When you come upon the golf course's parking lot on the right shore, your trip is nearly over. Look for the CT 185 bridge looming above. The take-out, whether you chose the Nod Road landing or the Pinchot Sycamore site, will be on the right.

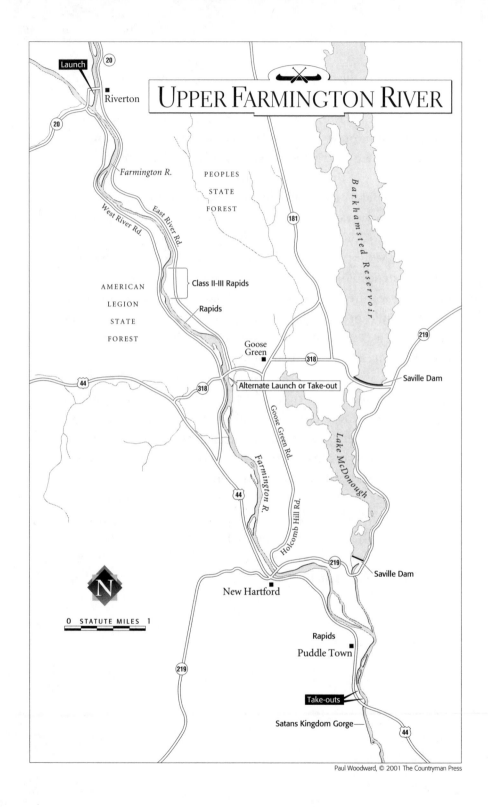

Launch

⑳ Riverton

✕ UPPER FARMINGTON RIVER

⑳

Farmington R.

PEOPLES
STATE
FOREST

West River Rd.

East River Rd.

Barkhamsted Reservoir

⒅①

Class II-III Rapids

AMERICAN
LEGION
STATE
FOREST

Rapids

Goose
Green

318

⑷⑷

318

Alternate Launch or Take-out

Saville Dam

219

Goose Green Rd.

Farmington R.

Lake McDonough

Holcomb Hill Rd.

⑷⑷

219

Saville Dam

N

0 STATUTE MILES 1

New Hartford

219

Rapids

Puddle Town

219

Take-outs

Satans Kingdom Gorge

⑷⑷

Paul Woodward, © 2001 The Countryman Press

27

Upper Farmington River

Riverton to Satan's Kingdom

Put-in Point	Take-out Points	Approximate Distance	Approximate Trip Time	Condition of Water	Portages
Riverton picnic area	CT 318 bridge	4½ miles	2 hours	Brief rapids, smooth	None
Riverton picnic area	Above US 44 bridge	9½ miles	3½–4 hours	Brief rapids, smooth stretches	None

Perhaps no stretch of any river in southern New England gets as much attention from outdoor enthusiasts in springtime as the upper reaches of the Farmington's West Branch. While fishermen wade into the water or cast from the banks, and hikers, campers, and picnickers prowl the shorelines, there is often a steady flow of adventurers floating down the river in canoes, kayaks, rubber rafts, and even inner tubes. There's good reason for the popularity of this segment of the Farmington, which lies in north-central Connecticut. The water is clean and fast, and there are numerous calm pools. The banks are covered with relatively unspoiled forests, yet there are roads for easy access, and facilities for picnicking and camping. Also, the area's proximity to Hartford makes it readily available to large numbers of people who seek a day in the "wilderness."

The stretch described here runs about 9½ miles, from Riverton to the US 44 bridge just above the famed gorge in the area between New Hartford and Canton called Satan's Kingdom. This trip is almost ideal from the canoeist's point of view. There is enough quickwater to make it challenging, and enough flatwater for relaxing breathers. There are islands to negotiate, and a few sets of rapids that require some whitewater skill. Yet, under normal water conditions for April and May, there is little real danger. Except for Satan's Kingdom, that is. This gorge lies a short distance below the US 44 bridge, so unless you are an accomplished whitewater canoeist, or you are traveling by tube or rubber raft, watch your river landmarks carefully.

The Farmington is another river in which water levels, and therefore the canoeing conditions, fluctuate considerably. Always check ahead through the Internet or by calling the Farmington River Watershed Association before starting out so that you'll know what to expect.

Access

Plan on taking out at Satan's Kingdom Recreation Area, just off US 44 above the bridge. And when you leave a car here, note the landmarks along the river—a huge rock in the center of the river and steps up the bank. Also, note the blue-roofed business complex across the highway from the parking area; in spring the roof is visible from the river. To be safe, it might be prudent to tie a flag or marker of some kind to a tree leaning over the water to make sure you don't miss the take-out. It may be difficult to pull out of the current if you go beyond these landmarks and pass under the bridge.

To reach the put-in, take US 44 north to CT 181, and then follow CT 181 north along the river all the way to CT 20 at Riverton. (For most of this section, there is a road running along the other side of the river also, so it is easy to scout the water by car before launching.) The best put-in at Riverton is from a state picnic area just west of the CT 20 bridge, across the highway from the well-known Hitchcock Chair Factory.

The River

The early going on the river is apt to be quite scratchy or riffly, with the best passage on the far right. Soon you'll experience what will become a familiar pattern, periods of rock-dodging followed by flat pools. Riffles, minor rapids, and pools alternate throughout much of this journey, with none lasting more than a few minutes at a time. You may also have

Rock-dodging is a big part of canoeing the upper Farmington.

to dodge fishing lines, for trout anglers flock to this area in spring in quest of the brown, brook, and rainbow trout that are stocked several times during the season. You will pass a popular picnic area on the left, part of Peoples State Forest, and a less visible recreation area on the right, the campground of American Legion State Forest. This campground is worth remembering if you are coming from any distance and plan to do the lower Farmington (see Trip 26) the next day.

After passing between old stone footbridge abutments, you will enter a pretty section featuring good patches of riffles and shorelines of hemlocks, birches, and laurel. You won't be able to see any roads from the water, but they run close to the river on both sides here, a comforting thought in case of a spill or some other problem. The first of many islands appears in this stretch; most can be skirted on either side. As a general rule in the early going, however, the right passages are shallower and wider, the left faster and rockier. As always, if you are new to quickwater canoeing, play it safe.

You should see wildlife along this river. Songbirds are common and so are ducks, mergansers, geese, kingfishers, sandpipers, and other waterbirds. In addition, you can see numerous beaver lodges along the shores and many signs of their gnawing on trees. Seeing the beavers themselves is less likely, though, because they do their work at night.

There are few rapids of real concern under normal water conditions, but you may occasionally find stretches that are Class II or even Class III in American Canoe Association ratings. Still, most can be negotiated by those with any whitewater experience. As noted, though, in times of high water, the complexion of the river changes considerably. At those times, only experts should be out on this river.

The first bridge you pass under is the iron span for CT 318—about 4½ miles and roughly 2 hours from the put-in. This area is the community of Pleasant Valley. There is a small put-in/take-out spot a short distance below the bridge on the left. From here to the next bridge, CT 219 at New Hartford, about 2½ miles downriver, the going is smoother with more flatwater than riffles. It takes only 45 minutes or less to reach the CT 219 bridge, beyond which you again encounter some rapids.

Just past the CT 219 bridge, in an area dominated by a high retaining wall on the right, the river is wide and rocky, and care must be taken in zigzagging between the boulders. Rock-dodging is the name of the game here. The rocks are big enough to give you and your canoe a good jolt if you hit them. Going around one island here can be a bit difficult in high water. Keep in mind also, as you leave New Hartford behind, that there is only one more bridge, a modern structure, to go under. After that one, the next bridge is US 44. If you miss your take-out, you'll go into the gorge at Satan's Kingdom, so start looking now for the landmarks that will tell you how close you are getting.

Among the first buildings on the right shore will be a restaurant. In just a few minutes more, the buildings of the River Run Apartments complex will appear on the right. This is the time to ease up on your paddling and watch the water ahead more closely. After passing through a "rock garden" of numerous boulders, look for a large boulder virtually alone in midstream, before the US 44 bridge comes into sight, then swing to the right to get out of the current. Now look for your flag and

Canoeists usually have to share the upper Farmington with anglers.

the steps up the bank. If you pass these markers and find yourself within sight of the high bridge, pull over to the right immediately. There is another small landing here, just upstream from the bridge. This is the last take-out spot before going into the gorge.

After landing, take a few minutes and follow a footpath under the bridge and along the river into Satan's Kingdom. High ledges tower above the water on both sides, and the river foams through a rocky chute. It's a splendid scene well worth the walk. But don't try taking a canoe through here. Leave that adventure for the rubber-raft and inner-tube enthusiasts.

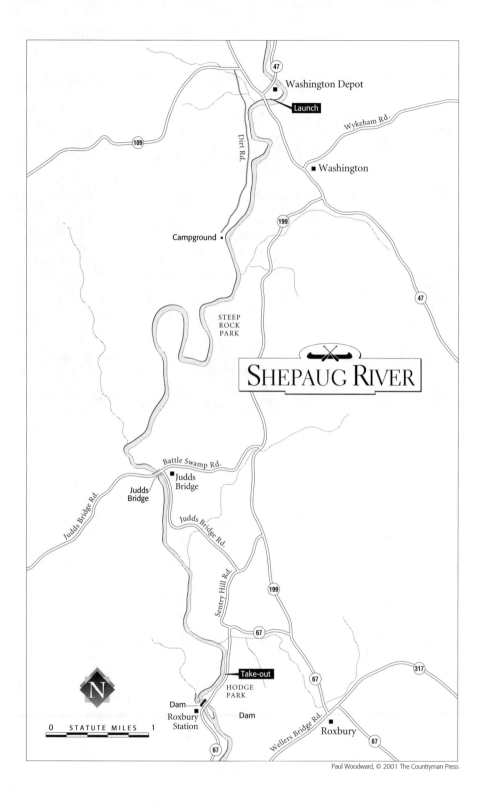

SHEPAUG RIVER

Washington Depot

Launch

Wykeham Rd.

Washington

Dirt Rd.

Campground

STEEP ROCK PARK

Battle Swamp Rd.

Judds Bridge

Judds Bridge

Judds Bridge Rd.

Judds Bridge Rd.

Sentry Hill Rd.

Take-out

HODGE PARK

Dam

Roxbury Station

Dam

Wellers Bridge Rd.

Roxbury

N

0 STATUTE MILES 1

Paul Woodward, © 2001 The Countryman Press

28

Shepaug River

Washington Depot to Roxbury Station

Put-in Point	Take-out Point	Approximate Distance	Approximate Trip Time	Condition of Water	Portages
CT 47 bridge	Hodge Park, CT 67	8 miles	3–3½ hours	Riffles, minor rapids	None

Fantastic scenery, miles of fast, clean water, and no dams or portages—that's the Shepaug River. One of the most beautiful runs in this book, or in all of southern New England for that matter, a trip down the Shepaug just might spoil you for tamer, less aesthetic outings. This river is hidden in the ancient hills of western Connecticut, but it's worth the drive to get there. Every canoeist with any quickwater skill at all should do the Shepaug at least once.

For the entire trip described here, an 8-mile stretch running from Washington Depot to a roadside park just north of Roxbury Station, the Shepaug offers riffles and minor rapids. This run is challenging enough to be fun, but not quite wild enough to be dangerous. And that's good, too, because for most of the trip the river runs through a stunning valley carved out of stone. At times the cliffs tower high above you. With this scenery to look at, it can be difficult to concentrate on the water. Unfortunately, the Shepaug is another springtime river. The water runs high and fast through March and early April. Then, by the end of April, it is usually so low it is unlikely you'll be able to make the run without a lot of scraping and scratching. However, occasionally it can be run later. We've done it in late May after a rainy spell and found the water conditions just about ideal.

Fast water and scenic shores make the Shepaug a canoeist's delight.

Access

To leave a car at the take-out point, take CT 67 (Exit 15 from I-84) north from Southbury through the village of Roxbury, and then follow it as it bends back south along the river, which will now be on your right. A roadside park called Hodge Park, which has picnic grills, provides the best access. CT 67 crosses the river, but do not go as far as the bridge. Taking out there is not easy. Moreover, a short distance above the bridge there is a dam and beyond the bridge is a notorious falls that invites disaster.

On your way to the put-in in Washington Depot, backtrack on CT 67. You can then take the first road left, Sentry Hill Road, for a look at the river a couple of miles upstream. Follow Sentry Hill Road to a bridge, known locally as Judd's Bridge, take a look at the water, and then return to CT 67. Or you can take a steep dirt road, Battle Swamp Road, uphill to the right to CT 67. Either way, once you're on CT 67, go left a short distance to CT 199, turn left (north), and drive to the picturesque village of Washington. There, turn left on CT 47 and drive the mile to the bridge over the Shepaug at Washington Depot. Just beyond the bridge, a street, Titus Road, runs to the right along the river. The put-in is about a hundred yards down this road from the parking lot of an office building. Park in the far right corner of the lot.

The River

The early part of this trip is somewhat indicative of what is to come. Good current, shallow water, and a bed of thousands of rocks—the word *Shepaug* means "rocky river"—combine to produce riffles that are a joy to skim over when there is enough water. It will be scratchy here in low water, however. You will leave the village of Washington Depot quickly, although a few houses can be seen along the river for a short distance. A feature of most of this run, impressive stands of hemlock trees, covers the left bank. You will probably see more hemlocks on this trip than on any other in this book.

Just as you swing around the first bend, you will float into a set of rapids, perhaps Class II in American Canoe Association ratings. In addition, there are a few other boulder patches to negotiate, but for the most part this early stretch is a quick and easy float. You will pass under the first bridge in a matter of 20 minutes or so, and then come upon a parklike area. This area, among southern New England's most beautiful spots with towering hemlocks casting a permanent shadow over moss-covered ledges, belongs to the Steep Rock Association. Also in this area is the Institute for American Indian Studies. The institute, which is located in the woods on the left side of the river and cannot be seen from the water, exhibits numerous Indian artifacts, a great many of which were found near here. The main entrance to the institute is on CT 199. Throughout the Steep Rock area, the Shepaug offers stretches of easy riffles punctuated by brief rapids. All can be run without scouting ahead when the water is high enough. The most difficult spot lies in a sharp bend where the right bank rises into an awesome moss-draped ledge. A couple of big boulders in the river here can catch unwary canoeists, but you should be able to get through if you stay just right of center. Almost immediately there is another, longer stretch of rapids. This time the best route is a straight run along the right bank. Then you will be back to alternate patches of riffles and short Class I rapids. None are difficult. Take advantage of one of the quieter segments here to pull ashore for a lunch break among the hemlocks, ferns, and chickadees.

After a series of bends that describe almost a full circle, the highest ledge of the river looms above you on the right. This immense rock is indeed steep—even hemlocks have trouble growing on the wall. The crest of the ledge is very high above the water. It's an inspiring sight, but don't spend all of your time looking up, for you are now entering the longest rapids of the trip. This stretch of whitewater extends several hundred yards and is very fast, but not difficult. Just great fun.

As the ridge on the right begins to flatten out, you will notice NO TRESPASSING signs—respect them—and fewer rapids. It is not far now to the next landmark, Judd's Bridge, the final bridge on this run. Just beyond the bridge, on the right, is a large cattle farm. The road on the left is Sentry Hill Road, which you drove earlier when you looked over the river. The valley widens now, and you'll find some oaks, maples, and sycamores along the banks. The ever-present hemlocks can still be seen cloaking the hillsides beyond.

Where the river divides around a big island, it is better to go right. The left passage is shorter, but also narrower and shallower, so you are more likely to get hung up there. And on this river, who wants to take shortcuts anyway? It is only a short distance to your car from the island. You'll probably wish you were just starting out instead of taking out.

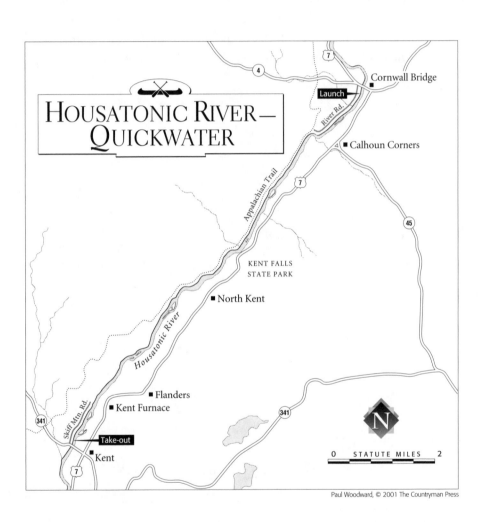

HOUSATONIC RIVER— QUICKWATER

Cornwall Bridge

Launch

River Rd.

Calhoun Corners

Appalachian Trail

KENT FALLS STATE PARK

North Kent

Housatonic River

Flanders

Kent Furnace

Skiff Mtn. Rd.

Take-out

Kent

N

0   STATUTE MILES   2

Paul Woodward, © 2001 The Countryman Press

29

Housatonic River—Quickwater

Cornwall Bridge to Kent

Put-in Point	Take-out Point	Approximate Distance	Approximate Trip Time	Condition of Water	Portages
Cornwall Bridge	CT 341 bridge	9½ miles	3–3½ hours	Mostly fast, some rapids	None

Do this stretch of the Housatonic River in northwestern Connecticut when the water is just right—not too high or too low—and you are likely to be hooked on canoeing for life. This 9½-mile trip has just about everything canoeists seek: enough fast current and rapids for excitement, and periods of calm that allow for relaxed gazing at the shorelines. The shores, too, are made to order with boulders, ledges, and virtually unbroken forest the entire distance of the trip. High wooded hills form the horizons on both sides of the river.

Unlike the Housatonic just a few miles upriver (see Trip 30), however, the section covered here—from Cornwall Bridge west of Cornwall to the town of Kent—undergoes great changes with the seasons, weather conditions, and dam releases. It should never be taken lightly, especially by those not skilled at handling whitewater. In spring and after heavy rainstorms, the river here can be wild and dangerous. One drop about a mile from the launch site is difficult enough to be rated Class III or more in high water, and another stretch of rapids late in the trip can be hazardous. In autumn and in extremely dry periods, on the other hand, it can be quite scratchy because of many nearly exposed rocks. The upper Housatonic, even though just a few miles away, remains gentle in all but flooding periods because of the huge dam at

Falls Village. Another section, between Falls Village and Cornwall, which includes a picturesque covered bridge at West Cornwall, is a favorite of whitewater canoeists. That segment is not included here because it requires skills beyond those of the average paddler and also because it cannot be run at all during low-water months.

As a bonus, the area of this trip is well provided with campgrounds and picnic areas—Housatonic Meadows State Park (near your start) north of Cornwall, the Macedonia Brook State Park (near the take-out) west of Kent, and the Kent Falls State Park, in between on US 7. All do a thriving business during prime canoeing time. After a day on the Housatonic, you'll know why. This is a river you will not want to leave.

Access

To make the Cornwall Bridge-to-Kent trip, drive US 7 to the village of Kent, go west on CT 341 a short distance to the river, then turn right onto Skiff Mountain Road immediately after crossing the bridge. This area belongs to the Kent School, and the school's dock is virtually below the bridge. Canoeists may use the dock as long as they do not interfere with school activities and if they park vehicles farther up the road near the school's tennis courts.

To reach the put-in, return to US 7. Turn north (left) and drive the 8 miles to Cornwall Bridge, where the highway joins CT 4 and turns west over the river. Immediately after crossing the bridge, turn right onto River Road, which swings down under the bridge at the river's shore. You can put in across from a state highway garage if you are careful to park your car out of the way of the state trucks.

The River

The Housatonic at the put-in is typical of the stretch you will be canoeing. It is wide, shallow, and rocky. There is no single channel. Moreover, during times of relatively low water you will have to start rock-dodging right away. The current is normally quick but generally not so swift that it cannot be handled. The river is wide enough to allow

Your canoe may take in water going over the drop at Swift's Bridge.

you to maneuver around rocks that you cannot float over. In the early going, these patches of riffles alternate with stretches of smooth water. Then, about a mile from the start, as you sweep around bends, the water drops over a ledge in the riverbed, and care must be taken in going over. Years ago a bridge spanned the river here, and the area is still known as the Swift's Bridge site. In high water, there are standing waves. In low water, a liftover may be required. I've floated this drop when it was nothing to be concerned about, and I've done it when it was a wild run indeed. Be prepared. Shortly beyond this ledge, as you round another bend, you will come upon a short rapid between larger rocks. It can be fun to run, but do it on the right.

This is perhaps the most beautiful portion of a truly beautiful river. Tall sycamores, maples, and oaks crowd the shoreline, along with some pines, beeches, and dogwoods. Huge boulders flank the river, particularly on the right, inviting you ashore for lunch or rest breaks. Take a break where you find trails coming down to the water from the right.

If you follow the paths back into the woods a few yards, you'll emerge on a well-worn lane. This is a segment of the famed Appalachian Trail that extends from Maine to Georgia. The trail follows the river here for a couple of miles, and a stroll along it provides a pleasant interlude. One spot in particular, marked by a brook entering the river from the right, is worth exploring for its extensive stonework in fences, retaining walls, and cellar holes. These remains date from the early days of life on the Housatonic. Today the area belongs to the birds and the squirrels.

Back on the river, you'll resume alternating between rock-dodging and easy paddling. Here the smooth stretches become longer, and you'll have more time to take in the scenery. Hawks and ospreys keep watch from the treetops, and during migration times—spring and fall—ducks and geese often congregate in this area. Floating into a flock of 60 Canada geese on one October trip was the highlight of the day for us. And seeing them clamber off into the sky against a backdrop of wine-red hillside foliage more than made up for all the low-water lining we had to do.

The water can be especially shallow around the several islands you'll pass. When you begin to see houses on the right shore, the first buildings of any kind since put-in, you are nearing the longest and best (or worst, depending on your point of view) rapids of the trip. Large rocks lie scattered across the river, and hundreds of smaller ones rest just below the surface. Experts may be able to run the full distance without hitting a rock, but most canoeists will bounce off a few here and there. Fortunately, only in high water is this stretch dangerous. At other times it's just fun.

The remaining ½ mile is almost anticlimactic. It is all smooth water as you approach the take-out at the Kent School dock on the right at the CT 341 bridge.

30

Housatonic River — Flatwater

Ashley Falls to Falls Village

Put-in Point	Take-out Point	Approximate Distance	Approximate Trip Time	Condition of Water	Portages
MA 7A bridge	Falls Village dam	10$\frac{1}{4}$ miles	4$\frac{1}{2}$–5 hours	Smooth	Old Canaan Dam

It would be a good idea before making this trip to read the books *This Hill, This Valley* or *Beyond Your Doorstep* by the late naturalist Hal Borland, for this stretch of the Housatonic River runs through the valley he so richly describes. Knowing a bit about the trees, plants, and animals along the river will greatly enhance the enjoyment of this leisurely 10$\frac{1}{4}$-mile trip.

You are likely to see otter slides and oriole nests, squirrels in the treetops, swallows over the water, dragonflies hovering above your paddle, ducks hiding in the weeds, mighty maples resplendent in autumn finery, and fragile wildflowers blooming on grassy banks. Borland, whose home you pass midway in the trip, described them all; finding them on your own is like following a treasure map.

This segment of the river, running from just above the Connecticut line in southwestern Massachusetts to Falls Village in Connecticut, is vastly different from another stretch of the Housatonic just a few miles to the south (see Trip 29). There the Housatonic is a fast and often wild whitewater river. For this entire section, however, except briefly during spring thaws, it is a tranquil waterway that wanders through a farming valley carved into the foothills of the Berkshires. Even the most inexperienced canoeist will be able to handle this portion of the river. There

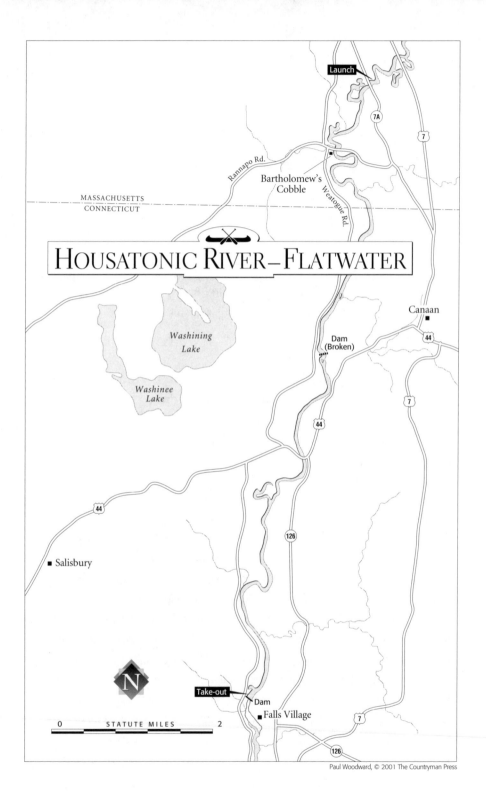

Launch

7A

7

Rannapo Rd.

MASSACHUSETTS
CONNECTICUT

Bartholomew's
Cobble

Weatogue Rd.

HOUSATONIC RIVER–FLATWATER

Canaan

44

*Washining
Lake*

Dam
(Broken)

*Washinee
Lake*

7

44

126

44

■ Salisbury

N

Take-out

Dam
■ Falls Village

7

0   STATUTE MILES   2

126

is one portage, around or over a broken dam, but this is a small price to pay for $4\frac{1}{2}$ to 5 hours of floating pleasure.

The put-in for this trip is also the take-out for still another segment of the Housatonic covered in this book (see Trip 1), and the two runs can be combined, but that would make for a float of more than 18 miles, with few opportunities for alternative take-outs. It is better to paddle each section separately; each has its own rewards.

Access

To leave a car at your take-out point, drive to Falls Village on CT 126, take Main Street to Water Street, go past a power station, cross the river, and then turn right onto Housatonic River Road and continue until you come to a landing beside the power-plant dam. This dam creates the smooth water of the trip you are undertaking.

Return with your canoe to CT 126, follow it north to US 44, and take that highway into Canaan. Here, pick up US 7, heading north, and follow it until reaching MA 7A, which angles off to the left, just south of the Massachusetts line. Stay on MA 7A for 2 miles, passing through Ashley Falls. At the river you will find parking space for a few cars just beyond the bridge. The best put-in is over a guardrail on the right.

The River

After floating under the bridge and a railroad bridge beside it, you'll begin to meander through a series of pastures interrupted by small woodlots. Cattle grazing beneath tall sycamores combine with farmhouses in the distance and wooded hills beyond to form an idyllic setting. You will find the water almost mirror smooth, but there will be enough current to keep you moving. In less than a mile, you will reach a modern concrete bridge (difficult access) and just beyond that, on the right, the rocky bluffs of Bartholomew's Cobble. This is an intriguing area of knolls and dense forests owned by a conservation group. Public trails wind through the property; you are likely to see hikers here, particularly in the spring and fall.

The Housatonic flows past the home of the late naturalist, Hal Borland.

The view of the cobble from the river is good at this point, but you will see its ledges and trees even better after completing a big oxbow bend that takes you around an open field and back toward the cobble. From this far side, especially in autumn, the bluffs are beautiful. A mixture of white birches, pines, maples, and oaks offer a delightful foliage display.

Once you leave the cobble behind, the shorelines flatten out into farming fields behind a screen of trees. The river runs wide and smooth here with a few logs and snags, but there is plenty of room to maneuver. Begin looking in this area for otter slides, well-worn paths used by the playful animals in their evening frolicking. You might be lucky enough to see an otter, but it is more likely you'll have to settle for the slides and footprints in the mud. A search along the shoreline may turn up other tracks, too—deer, raccoon, fox, muskrat, mink, and skunk—for this valley has an abundance of wildlife.

Shortly after passing an abandoned stone abutment in the middle of the river, look for a large weeping willow on the right bank. This is the only large willow in the area. Just beyond the willow is a bench near the water and, behind that, facing the river, stands the red Borland house. It is easily seen from the river. Also visible are the sloping fields and hillsides of Borland's books. Do not leave the river here, however, for the banks are private property.

About ½ mile past the Borland farm, you'll come to the old broken Canaan Dam. In high water, you might be able to run over the collapsed right end. The portage path is through the woods on the left. This can be a relatively tough carry, however, so if the water is calm you might be better off just floating up to the center of the dam, lifting over it, carrying across the small island that has formed below the dam, and then putting in again. We have done this without major difficulties.

Your next landmark, less than a mile past the broken dam, is the US 44 bridge (no easy access), about 6½ miles from the start. After this point, the river slows down even more. It may take you 2 hours to paddle the final 4 miles. Unless you are in a hurry you won't mind, because the attractiveness of the shores increases as the valley narrows and the hills draw closer on both sides. Some of the hills are so high that the houses at their bottom, easily seen from the water, are in shadow by midafternoon. When you begin finding boulders in the riverbed and seeing ledges on shore, you'll be nearing the Falls Village dam. The take-out is on the right.

Index